Dimensions Math
Textbook 2B

Authors and Reviewers

Bill Jackson

Jenny Kempe

Cassandra Turner

Allison Coates

Tricia Salerno

Pearly Yuen

Consultant

Dr. Richard Askey

Singapore Math Inc.

Published by Singapore Math Inc.

19535 SW 129th Avenue
Tualatin, OR 97062
www.singaporemath.com

Dimensions Math® Textbook 2B
ISBN 978-1-947226-07-4

First published 2018
Reprinted 2019, 2020

Printed in China

Acknowledgments

Editing by the Singapore Math Inc. team.
Design and illustration by Cameron Wray with Carli Fronius.

Preface

The Dimensions Math® Pre-Kindergarten to Grade 5 series is based on the pedagogy and methodology of math education in Singapore. The curriculum develops concepts in increasing levels of abstraction, emphasizing the three pedagogical stages: Concrete, Pictorial, and Abstract. Each topic is introduced, then thoughtfully developed through the use of problem solving, student discourse, and opportunities for mastery of skills.

Features and Lesson Components

Students work through the lessons with the help of five friends: Emma, Alex, Sofia, Dion, and Mei. The characters appear throughout the series and help students develop metacognitive reasoning through questions, hints, and ideas.

The colored boxes ▮ and blank lines in the textbook lessons are used to facilitate student discussion. Rather than writing in the textbooks, students can use whiteboards or notebooks to record their ideas, methods, and solutions.

Chapter Opener

Each chapter begins with an engaging scenario that stimulates student curiosity in new concepts. This scenario also provides teachers an opportunity to review skills.

Think

Students, with guidance from teachers, solve a problem using a variety of methods.

Learn

One or more solutions to the problem in **Think** are presented, along with definitions and other information to consolidate the concepts introduced in **Think**.

Do

A variety of practice problems allow teachers to lead discussion or encourage independent mastery. These activities solidify and deepen student understanding of the concepts.

Exercise

A pencil icon ──────────▶ at the end of the lesson links to additional practice problems in the workbook.

Practice

Periodic practice provides teachers with opportunities for consolidation, remediation, and assessment.

Review

Cumulative reviews provide ongoing practice of concepts and skills.

| Emma | Alex | Sofia | Dion | Mei |

Contents

Chapter	Lesson	Page

Chapter	Lesson	Page

Chapter 8

Mental Calculation

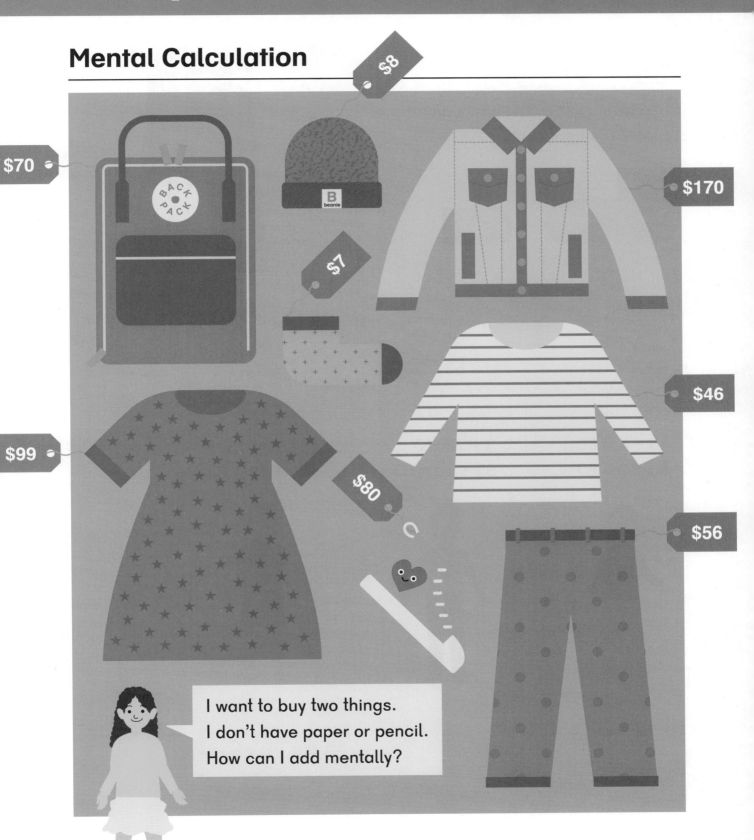

$8

$70

$170

$7

$46

$99

$80

$56

I want to buy two things.
I don't have paper or pencil.
How can I add mentally?

Think

Sofia wants to buy the pants and the socks.
What is the total cost?

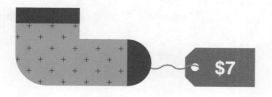

$56

$7

Learn

56 + 7

4   3

56 + 4 = 60
60 + 3 = 63

56 + 7

53   3

3 + 7 = 10
53 + 10 = 63

56 + 7

50   6

6 + 7 = 13
50 + 13 = 63

56 + 7 =

The total cost is $.

Do

1 (a) Add 45 and 4.

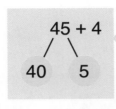 

45 + 4 = ▢

(b) Add 67 and 5.

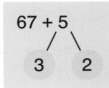 

67 + 5 = ▢

2 (a) Add 618 and 3.

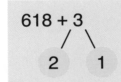 

618 + 3 = ▢

(b) Add 5 and 435.

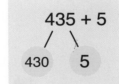 

5 + 435 = ▢

Did you use a different method?

3 Find the value mentally.

(a) 46 + 3

(b) 34 + 6

(c) 27 + 8

(d) 84 + 7

(e) 3 + 84

(f) 7 + 25

(g) 372 + 5

(h) 441 + 7

(i) 446 + 7

(j) 843 + 9

(k) 5 + 333

(l) 6 + 166

Exercise 1 · page 1

Lesson 2
Adding Tens Mentally

Think

Mei's sister wants to buy the jacket and the shoes.
How much will she pay?

$80

$170

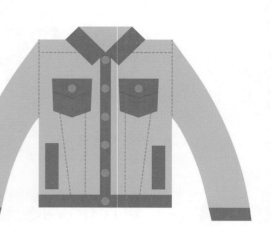

Learn

170 + 80
  /   \
 30   50

170 + 30 = 200
200 + 50 = 250

170 + 80
  /   \
150   20

20 + 80 = 100
150 + 100 = 250

170 + 80
  /   \
100   70

70 + 80 = 150
100 + 150 = 250

170 + 80
17 tens + 8 tens = 25 tens
25 tens = 250

170 + 80 = ▨

Mei's sister will pay $▨ .

Do

1 (a) Add 230 and 40.

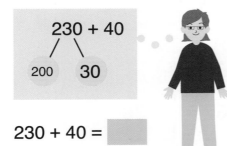

$230 + 40 =$ ▢

(b) Add 352 and 30.

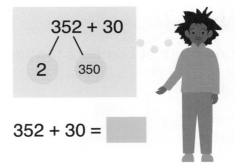

$352 + 30 =$ ▢

(c) Add 350 and 60.

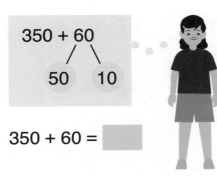

$350 + 60 =$ ▢

(d) Add 564 and 70.

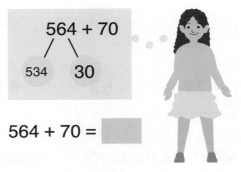

$564 + 70 =$ ▢

2 Add 75 and 80.

$75 + 80 =$ ▢

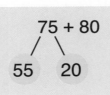

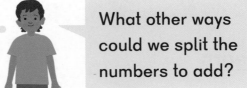

What other ways could we split the numbers to add?

3 Find the value mentally.

(a) $420 + 60$

(b) $630 + 70$

(c) $137 + 50$

(d) $56 + 40$

(e) $540 + 80$

(f) $60 + 375$

(g) $84 + 50$

(h) $60 + 92$

(i) $80 + 672$

Exercise 2 • page 3

Think

Find pairs of numbers that make 100.

43	64	45	26	36
24	54	35	56	74
65	23	33	76	67
77	55	44	57	46

What are the totals of the tens and the ones
of each pair of numbers that make 100?

Learn

$$50 + 40 = \boxed{}$$

$$7 + 3 = \boxed{}$$

	tens	ones
5	tens	7 ones
+ 4	tens	3 ones
☐	tens	☐ ones

How many tens and how
many ones are there?

$$57 + 43 = \boxed{}$$

Do

1 What number must be added to 62 to get 100?

10 10 10 10 10   1   1
10

62 + [ ] = 100

How many more tens and ones will make 9 tens and 10 ones?

2 Find the missing number.

(a) 85 + [ ] = 100

(b) 39 + [ ] = 100

(c) 73 + [ ] = 100

(d) [ ] + 66 = 100

(e) [ ] + 7 = 100

(f) [ ] + 14 = 100

3 Find the value.

(a) 100 − 84

(b) 100 − 77

(c) 100 − 58

(d) 100 − 9

(e) 100 − 45

(f) 100 − 24

4 Sara wants to save $100 to buy a new coat.
She has already saved $48.
How much more does she need to save?

Exercise 3 • page 5

Think

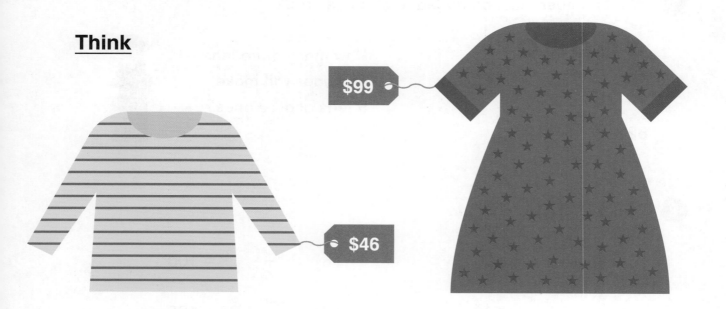

Mei's dad wants to buy her the shirt and the dress.
How much will he pay?

Learn

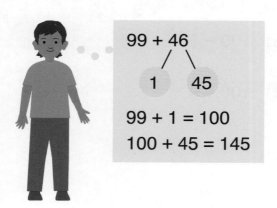

99 + 46

1   45

99 + 1 = 100
100 + 45 = 145

46 + 99
99 is 1 less than 100.
46 + 100 = 146
146 − 1 = 145
Adding 100 and
subtracting 1 is the
same as adding 99.

46 + 99 =

He will pay $.

Do

1 (a) Add 99 and 57.

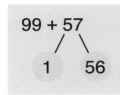

99 + 57
/ \
1   56

99 + 57 =

(b) Add 65 and 98.

65 + 100 − 2

65 + 98 =

2 (a) Add 611 and 98.

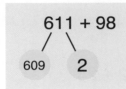

611 + 98
/ \
609   2

611 + 98 =

(b) Add 246 and 97.

246 + 100 − 3

246 + 97 =

What method did you use?

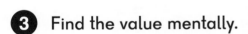

3 Find the value mentally.

(a) 99 + 7

(b) 5 + 98

(c) 98 + 67

(d) 53 + 99

(e) 84 + 97

(f) 99 + 98

(g) 347 + 99

(h) 524 + 98

(i) 97 + 305

(j) 97 + 617

(k) 99 + 699

(l) 201 + 98

Exercise 4 · page 7

1 (a) $62 +$ ▢ $= 100$ (b) ▢ $+ 26 = 100$

(c) $100 - 87 =$ ▢   (d) $100 -$ ▢ $= 51$

2 Find the value mentally.

(a) $43 + 5$ (b) $47 + 6$

(c) $8 + 69$ (d) $7 + 73$

(e) $66 + 30$ (f) $72 + 24$

(g) $23 + 77$ (h) $87 + 50$

(i) $65 + 98$ (j) $99 + 88$

3 Find the value mentally.

(a) $165 + 4$ (b) $553 + 9$

(c) $8 + 468$ (d) $70 + 112$

(e) $123 + 231$ (f) $250 + 30$

(g) $481 + 60$ (h) $819 + 90$

(i) $898 + 99$ (j) $97 + 427$

4 A snowboard costs $149.
A pair of skis costs $9 more than the snowboard.
How much does the pair of skis cost?

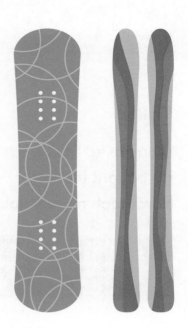

5 Pekelo wants to buy a keyboard piano.
He has saved $348.
He needs to save another $60 to buy the piano.
How much does the piano cost?

6 Mrs. Clark drove 98 miles on Saturday
and 74 miles on Sunday.
How many miles did she drive altogether?

7 Mr. Jung drove 100 miles on Monday,
47 miles on Tuesday, and 99 miles on Wednesday.
How far did he drive in all?

8 Suitcase A weighs 58 lb.
Suitcase B weighs 40 lb more than Suitcase A.

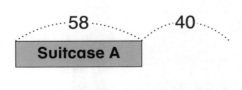

(a) How much does Suitcase B weigh?

(b) How much do both suitcases weigh together?

Exercise 5 • page 9

Think

Dion saved $62.

He bought the hat.

How much money does he have left?

Learn

$$62 - 8$$

52   10

$10 - 8 = 2$
$52 + 2 = 54$

$$62 - 8$$

2   60

$60 - 8 = 52$
$2 + 52 = 54$

$$62 - 8$$

2   6

$62 - 2 = 60$
$60 - 6 = 54$

$$62 - 8$$

50   12

$12 - 8 = 4$
$50 + 4 = 54$

$62 - 8 = $

Dion has left.

Do

1   (a)   Subtract 5 from 38.

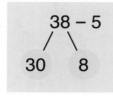

38 − 5

30   8

38 − 5 = ▢

(b)   Subtract 7 from 81.

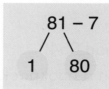

81 − 7

1   80

81 − 7 = ▢

2   (a)   Subtract 8 from 430.

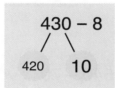

430 − 8

420   10

430 − 8 = ▢

(b)   Subtract 7 from 305.

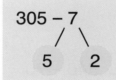

305 − 7

5   2

305 − 7 = ▢

3   Find the value mentally.

(a)   50 − 5   (b)   53 − 5   (c)   48 − 6

(d)   80 − 7   (e)   82 − 7   (f)   41 − 9

(g)   245 − 8   (h)   240 − 8   (i)   669 − 3

(j)   700 − 6   (k)   702 − 6   (l)   376 − 9

Exercise 6 • page 13

Think

Alex's brother had $540.
He spent $70 on a backpack.
How much money does he have left?

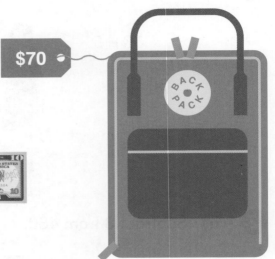

$70

Learn

540 − 70

440   100

100 − 70 = 30
440 + 30 = 470

540 − 70

40   500

500 − 70 = 430
40 + 430 = 470

540 − 70

40   30

540 − 40 = 500
500 − 30 = 470

540 − 70
54 tens − 7 tens = 47 tens
47 tens = 470

540 − 70 = [   ]

He has $ [   ] left.

Do

1 (a) Subtract 50 from 680.

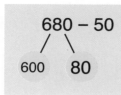

680 – 50 = [ ]

(b) Subtract 80 from 350.

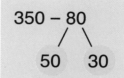

350 – 80 = [ ]

(c) Subtract 70 from 510.

510 – 70 = [ ]

(d) Subtract 40 from 329.

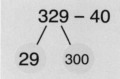

329 – 40 = [ ]

2 Find the value mentally.

(a) 90 – 50

(b) 82 – 30

(c) 180 – 40

(d) 530 – 30

(e) 300 – 40

(f) 320 – 40

(g) 900 – 80

(h) 940 – 80

(i) 945 – 80

(j) 160 – 70

(k) 527 – 60

(l) 655 – 60

Exercise 7 • page 15

Think

Sofia's cousin had $340.

She spent $99 on a guitar.

How much money does she have left?

Learn

340 − 99

240   100

100 − 99 = 1

240 + 1 = 241

340 − 99 = [ ]

She has $[ ] left.

99 is 1 less than 100.

340 − 100 = 240

240 + 1 = 241

Subtracting 100 and adding 1 is the same as subtracting 99.

Do

1 (a) Subtract 98 from 800.

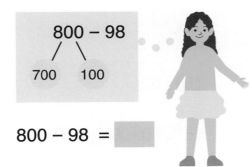

$$800 - 98$$
700   100

$$800 - 98 = \boxed{}$$

(b) Subtract 99 from 500.

$$500 - 100 + 1$$

$$500 - 99 = \boxed{}$$

2 (a) Subtract 98 from 405.

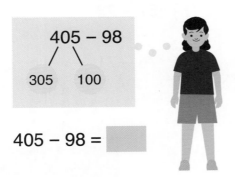

$$405 - 98$$
305   100

$$405 - 98 = \boxed{}$$

(b) Subtract 97 from 562.

$$562 - 100 + 3$$

$$562 - 97 = \boxed{}$$

3 Find the value mentally.

(a) $700 - 99$

(b) $200 - 98$

(c) $900 - 97$

(d) $406 - 98$

(e) $305 - 98$

(f) $508 - 99$

(g) $320 - 99$

(h) $560 - 97$

(i) $770 - 98$

(j) $544 - 98$

(k) $188 - 99$

(l) $333 - 97$

Exercise 8 · page 17

1 Find the value mentally.

(a) 57 – 5

(b) 62 – 7

(c) 84 – 6

(d) 70 – 9

(e) 80 – 60

(f) 95 – 50

(g) 58 – 40

(h) 67 – 23

(i) 87 – 15

(j) 75 – 71

2 There are 41 children in the water
at swimming practice.
8 children get out of the water.
How many children are still in the water?

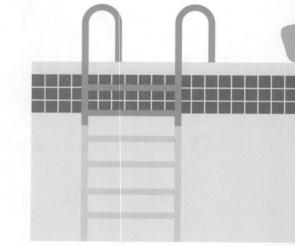

3 Micah weighs 98 lb.
He weighs 30 lb more than Holly.
How much does Holly weigh?

98 lb

Micah

Holly

? 30 lb

4 Find the value mentally.

(a) 568 – 5

(b) 450 – 4

(c) 260 – 5

(d) 342 – 8

(e) 130 – 50

(f) 560 – 90

(g) 600 – 98

(h) 507 – 99

(i) 822 – 97

(j) 227 – 98

(k) 999 – 123

(l) 789 – 18

5 There are 420 children in the school band.
80 of them are second graders.
How many children in the band are not
second graders?

6 Adriana had $400.
After she bought a bass drum, she had $98 left.
How much did the drum cost?

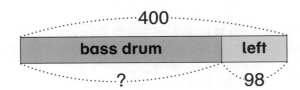

1 Find the value mentally.

(a) 85 + 7

(b) 85 – 7

(c) 85 + 70

(d) 85 – 70

(e) 230 + 8

(f) 230 – 8

(g) 230 + 80

(h) 230 – 80

(i) 408 + 98

(j) 408 – 98

(k) 732 + 99

(l) 732 – 99

2 (a) What number is 6 more than 789?

(b) What number is 70 less than 430?

(c) What number is 36 less than 100?

3 (a) 43 + ▮ = 56

(b) 85 – ▮ = 71

(c) ▮ + 80 = 472

(d) 62 + ▮ = 161

(e) 100 – 87 = ▮

(f) ▮ – 45 = 55

(g) 137 – ▮ = 38

(h) ▮ – 50 = 227

4 What sign, >, <, or =, goes in the ◯?

(a) 235 + 9 ◯ 235 + 90

(b) 364 + 7 ◯ 367 + 4

(c) 432 + 7 ◯ 472 + 3

(d) 762 − 7 ◯ 267 + 7

(e) 580 + 60 ◯ 740 − 100

(f) 75 + 6 ◯ 100 − 30

(g) 23 + 98 ◯ 401 − 99

(h) 137 + 98 ◯ 333 − 98

5 A baker bought 63 lb of flour
and used 9 lb of the flour to make cakes.
How many pounds of flour does he have left?

6 After using 63 lb of flour to make cakes,
a baker has 9 lb of flour left.
How many pounds of flour did he have at first?

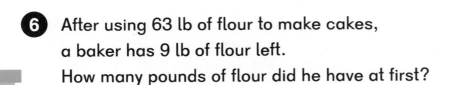

7 Starkist the goat weighs 134 lb.
Her sister Nutmeg weighs 6 lb more than she does.

(a) How much does Nutmeg weigh?

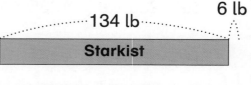

(b) How much do both goats
weigh altogether?

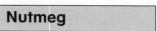

8 There were 95 men and 70 women at a show.
There were 80 fewer adults than children at the show.

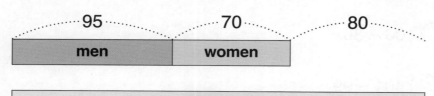

(a) How many adults were there?

(b) How many children were there?

9 A yellow ribbon is 240 cm long.
It is 90 cm longer than a green ribbon.

(a) How long is the green ribbon?

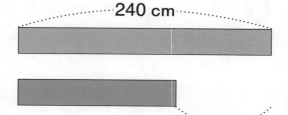

(b) What is the total length of
both ribbons together?

Exercise 10 • page 23

Chapter 9

Multiplication and Division of 3 and 4

Think

There are 3 trees in each planter.

$1 \times 3 = $

How many trees are there in ⬜ planters?

⬜ $\times 3 = ?$

How many trees are there in 2 planters?

Find the number of trees if there are ...

3 , 4 , 5 , 6 , 7 , 8 , 9 , and 10 planters.

How does the total number of trees change when the number of planters increases by 1?

Learn

+1 (
$1 \times 3 = 3$
———— +3 ———— +3 ————
$2 \times 3 = 6$

$3 \times 3 = 9$ 3×3 is [ ] more than 2×3.

$4 \times 3 = 12$ 4×3 is [ ] less than 5×3.

$5 \times 3 = 15$

$6 \times 3 = 18$

$7 \times 3 = 21$ 7×3 is 3 more than [ ] $\times 3$.

$8 \times 3 = 24$

$9 \times 3 = 27$ 9×3 is 3 less than [ ] $\times 3$.

$10 \times 3 = 30$

Look at the products.
If you add the digit in the ones place to the digit in the tens place,
what do you notice about the sums?

12: $1 + 2 = 3$,
15: $1 + 5 = 6$,
18: $1 + 8 = 9$,
21: $2 + 1 = 3$,
...

Do

1 Count by 3s to 30.

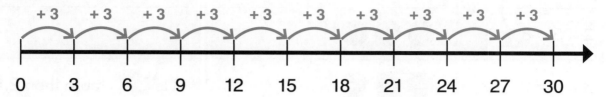

2 (a) $2 \times 3 = \boxed{}$ (b) $4 \times 3 = \boxed{}$

3 Use array dot cards to find the totals.

(a) $5 \times 3 = \boxed{}$ (b) $10 \times 3 = \boxed{}$

$6 \times 3 = \boxed{}$ $9 \times 3 = \boxed{}$

$7 \times 3 = \boxed{}$ $8 \times 3 = \boxed{}$

4 How much do 9 bags of balloons cost?

 $\boxed{} \times \boxed{} = \boxed{}$

9 bags cost $\$ \boxed{}$.

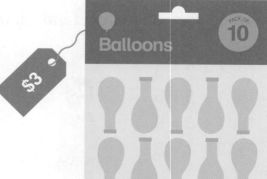

Exercise 1 • page 27

9-1 The Multiplication Table of 3

Think

How can we use multiplication to find the total number of rolls?

Learn

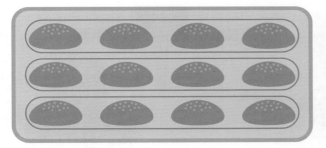 

$4 + 4 + 4 =$ ⬚ | $3 \times 4 =$ ⬚ $3 + 3 + 3 + 3 =$ ⬚ | $4 \times 3 =$ ⬚

$3 \times 4 = 4 \times 3$

We can use rows or columns.

There are ⬚ rolls altogether.

Do

1

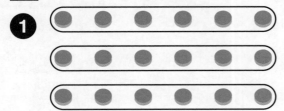 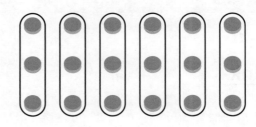

6 + 6 + 6 = ▢   3 + 3 + 3 + 3 + 3 + 3 = ▢

3 × 6 = ▢   6 × 3 = ▢

2 (a) 2 × 3 = ▢ × 2   (b) 7 × ▢ = 3 × 7

(c) 9 × 3 = 3 × ▢   (d) ▢ × 3 = 3 × 5

3

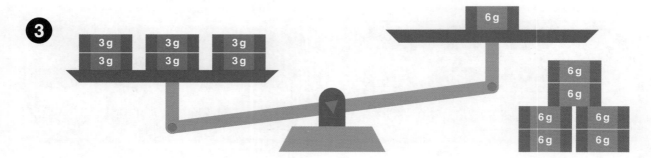

How many more of the 6-gram weights
do we need to make the scale balance?

4 Sophia's jacket has 3 rows of 3 pins.
How many pins are on the jacket?

▢ × ▢ = ▢

There are ▢ pins.

5 What is the value of each?

1 × 3	3 × 1
2 × 3	3 × 2
3 × 3	3 × 3
4 × 3	3 × 4
5 × 3	3 × 5
6 × 3	3 × 6
7 × 3	3 × 7
8 × 3	3 × 8
9 × 3	3 × 9
10 × 3	3 × 10

Make flash cards and practice the multiplication facts of 3.

3 × 8	24

Which facts did you already learn from the multiplication facts of 2, 5, and 10?

Think

There are 24 crayons.

(a) Put them equally into 3 cups.
How many are in each cup?

(b) Put 3 crayons in each cup.
How many cups are needed?

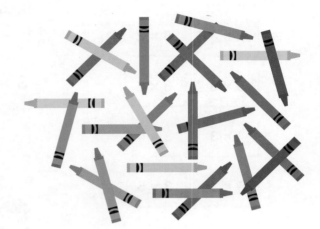

Learn

(a) Make 3 equal groups.

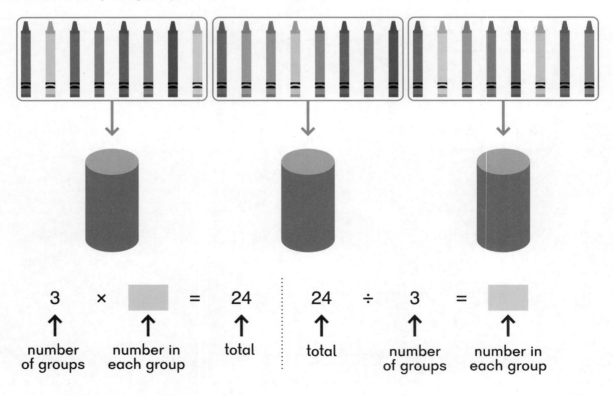

$$3 \quad \times \quad \boxed{} \quad = \quad 24 \qquad 24 \quad \div \quad 3 \quad = \quad \boxed{}$$

↑   ↑   ↑   ↑   ↑   ↑

number   number in   total   total   number   number in
of groups   each group   of groups   each group

There are 　　 crayons in each cup.

(b) Group by 3.

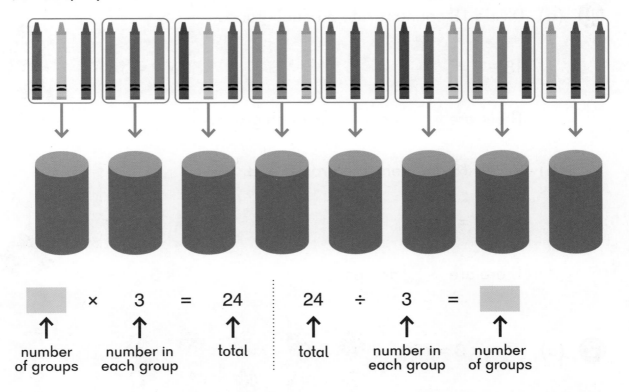

number of groups ↑ × 3 ↑ = 24 ↑   24 ↑ ÷ 3 ↑ = ↑

number of groups   number in each group   total   total   number in each group   number of groups

cups are needed.

To divide by 3, we can use the multiplication facts of 3.

Do

1 (a) Divide 18 counters into 3 equal groups.

$18 \div 3 = $ ____

$3 \times \; ? = 18$

There are ____ counters in each group.

(b) Divide 18 counters into groups of 3.

$18 \div 3 = $ ____

There are ____ groups.

$? \times 3 = 18$

2 (a) ____ $\times 3 = 15$

$15 \div 3 = $ ____

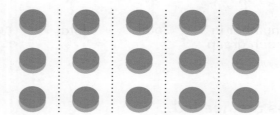

(b) $3 \times$ ____ $= 27$

$27 \div 3 = $ ____

3 Find the value.

(a) $21 \div 3$ (b) $12 \div 3$ (c) $6 \div 3$

(d) $30 \div 3$ (e) $9 \div 3$ (f) $24 \div 3$

Exercise 3 • page 31

1 (a) $4 \times 3 =$ ▢

(b) $3 \times 5 =$ ▢

(c) $2 \times 3 =$ ▢

(d) $3 \times 10 =$ ▢

(e) $9 \times 3 =$ ▢

(f) $3 \times 7 =$ ▢

(g) ▢ $\times 3 = 9$

(h) $3 \times$ ▢ $= 3$

(i) $18 =$ ▢ $\times 3$

2 Find the value.

(a) $6 \div 3$

(b) $24 \div 3$

(c) $15 \div 3$

(d) $27 \div 3$

(e) $9 \div 3$

(f) $21 \div 3$

(g) $18 \div 3$

(h) $30 \div 3$

(i) $12 \div 3$

3 A baseball costs $8.
How much do 3 baseballs cost?

4 Emma spent $9 on these balloons.
Each bag has 10 balloons.

(a) How many bags did she buy?

(b) How many balloons did she buy?

Lesson 5
The Multiplication Table of 4

Think

Dion is putting 4 stamps in each row in a stamp album.

1 × 4 = ☐

How many stamps are there in ☐ rows?

☐ × 4 = ?

How many stamps are there in 2 rows?

Find the number of stamps if there are...

3 , 4 , 5 , 6 , 7 , 8 , 9 , and 10 rows.

How does the total number of stamps change when the number of rows increases by 1?

Learn

$1 × 4 = 4$

+1

$2 × 4 = 8$

+4

+4

$3 × 4 = 12$

$4 × 4 = 16$ $4 × 4 = 5 × 4 -$ ▢

$5 × 4 = 20$

$6 × 4 = 24$ $6 × 4 = 5 × 4 +$ ▢

$7 × 4 = 28$ ▢ $× 4$ is 4 more than $6 × 4$.

$8 × 4 = 32$

$9 × 4 = 36$ ▢ $× 4 = 10 × 4 - 4$

$10 × 4 = 40$

I found $8 × 4$ this way:

$8 × 2 = 16$

$16 + 16 = 32$

So, $8 × 4 = 32$.

Do

1 Count by 4s to 40.

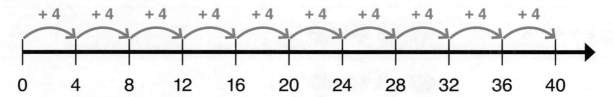

2 (a)  $2 \times 4 =$ ____ (b) 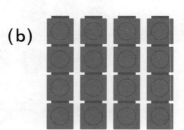 $4 \times 4 =$ ____

3 Use array dot cards to find the totals.

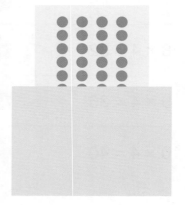

(a) $5 \times 4 =$ ____ (b) $10 \times 4 =$ ____

$6 \times 4 =$ ____ $9 \times 4 =$ ____

$7 \times 4 =$ ____ $8 \times 4 =$ ____

4 How much do 5 bags of party hats cost?

____ × ____ = ____

5 bags cost $ ____ .

Exercise 5 • page 39

9-5 The Multiplication Table of 4

Think

Multiply to find the total number of lights.

Learn

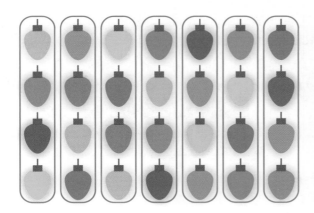

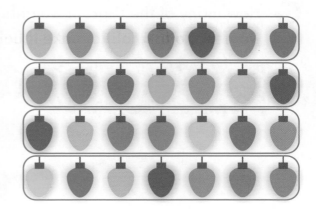

4 + 4 + 4 + 4 + 4 + 4 + 4 = ⬚

7 + 7 + 7 + 7 = ⬚

7 × 4 = ⬚

4 × 7 = ⬚

There are ⬚ lights.

7 × 4 = 4 × 7

Do

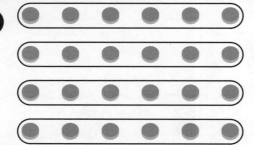

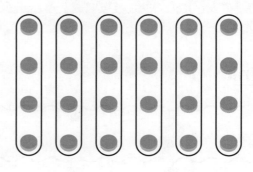

$6 + 6 + 6 + 6 =$ [ ]

$4 + 4 + 4 + 4 + 4 + 4 =$ [ ]

$4 \times 6 =$ [ ]

$6 \times 4 =$ [ ]

2 (a) $3 \times 4 =$ [ ] $\times 3$

(b) $8 \times$ [ ] $= 4 \times 8$

(c) $9 \times 4 = 4 \times$ [ ]

(d) [ ] $\times 4 = 4 \times 10$

3 How many of the 8-gram weights do
we need to take off to make it balance?

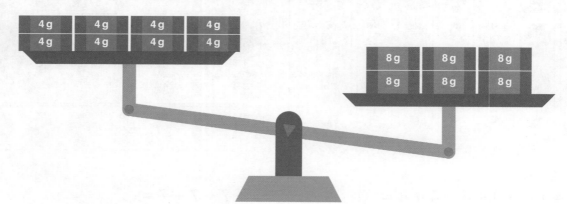

4 There are 9 spaces on a tic-tac-toe board.
How many spaces are on 4 boards?

4 groups of 9 = 9 groups of 4

$9 \times 4 = $ ⬜

There are ⬜ spaces on 4 boards.

5 What is the value of each?

1 × 4	4 × 1
2 × 4	4 × 2
3 × 4	4 × 3
4 × 4	4 × 4
5 × 4	4 × 5
6 × 4	4 × 6
7 × 4	4 × 7
8 × 4	4 × 8
9 × 4	4 × 9
10 × 4	4 × 10

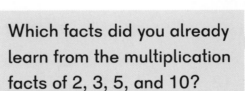

Make flash cards and practice
the multiplication facts of 4.

9 × 4	36

Which facts did you already
learn from the multiplication
facts of 2, 3, 5, and 10?

Exercise 6 • page 41

Think

There are 12 cookie twirls.

(a) Put them equally into 4 bags.
How many are in each bag?

(b) Put 4 twirls in each bag.
How many bags are needed?

Learn

(a) Make 4 equal groups.

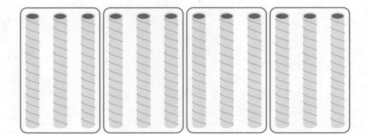

$4 \times$ ▢ $= 12$

$12 \div 4 =$ ▢

There are ▢ twirls in each bag.

(b) Group by 4.

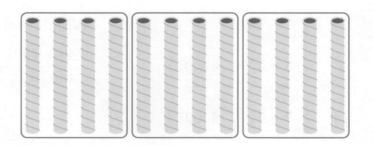

▢ $\times 4 = 12$

$12 \div 4 =$ ▢

▢ bags are needed.

Do

1 (a) Divide 20 counters into groups of 4.

$? \times 4 = 20$

$20 \div 4 = $ ⬜

There are ⬜ groups.

(b) Divide 20 counters into 4 groups.

$4 \times ? = 20$

$20 \div 4 = $ ⬜

There are ⬜ counters in each group.

2 (a) ⬜ $\times 4 = 24$

$24 \div 4 = $ ⬜

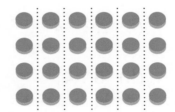

(b) $4 \times$ ⬜ $= 32$

$32 \div 4 = $ ⬜

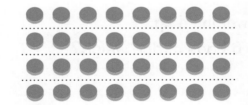
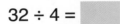

3 Find the value.

(a) $28 \div 4$ (b) $40 \div 4$ (c) $8 \div 4$

(d) $4 \div 4$ (e) $36 \div 4$ (f) $16 \div 4$

Exercise 7 · page 43

❶ (a) 4 × 6 = ▯

(b) 5 × 4 = ▯

(c) 8 × 4 = ▯

(d) 7 × 4 = ▯

(e) 9 × 4 = ▯

(f) 4 × 3 = ▯

(g) ▯ × 4 = 16

(h) 4 × ▯ = 40

(i) 8 = ▯ × 4

❷ Find the value.

(a) 28 ÷ 4

(b) 40 ÷ 4

(c) 16 ÷ 4

(d) 32 ÷ 4

(e) 12 ÷ 4

(f) 36 ÷ 4

(g) 20 ÷ 4

(h) 8 ÷ 4

(i) 24 ÷ 4

❸ A bag of rice weighs 4 kg.
How much do 6 bags of rice weigh?

❹ Sofia spent $16 on these party hats.

(a) How many bags did she buy?

(b) Each bag has 8 hats.
How many hats did she buy?

$4

Party Hats

PACK OF 8

5 A designer needs 5 m of cloth to make a dress. How many meters does she need for 4 dresses?

6 36 children are playing a game. They want to make teams of 4. How many teams can they make?

7 Benjamin wants to buy a remote control truck that costs $35. He saves $4 a week for 7 weeks.

   (a) How much money has he saved?

   (b) How much more money does he still need to save?

8 Aliya wants to cut a 22-ft long ribbon into pieces each 4 ft long.

   (a) Will she be able to use the entire length of ribbon?

   (b) How many pieces of ribbon that are each 4 ft long will she have?

   (c) How long will the left-over piece be?

Exercise 8 • page 47

1 Find the value.

(a) 8 × 4

(b) 7 × 5

(c) 5 × 3

(d) 9 × 2

(e) 4 × 10

(f) 9 × 3

(g) 7 × 4

(h) 7 × 3

(i) 9 × 4

(j) 12 ÷ 4

(k) 16 ÷ 2

(l) 30 ÷ 5

(m) 24 ÷ 3

(n) 40 ÷ 4

(o) 12 ÷ 2

(p) 16 ÷ 4

(q) 24 ÷ 4

(r) 60 ÷ 10

2 Jacob ran 25 miles in 5 days.
He ran the same number of miles each day.
How many miles did he run each day?

3 A store manager orders 4 bags of coffee.
Each bag has 10 lb of coffee.
A worker divides all the coffee to make
bags with 5 lb of coffee in each bag.

(a) How much coffee is there?

(b) How many 5-lb bags of
coffee will there be?

4 (a) $5 \times 3 = 3 + 3 + 3 + 3 +$ ▢   (b) $5 \times 3 = 3 + 3 + 3 +$ ▢

(c) $6 \times 4 = 4 + 4 + 4 +$ ▢   (d) $8 \times 2 = 2 + 2 +$ ▢

5 (a) $5 \times 4 =$ ▢ $\times 2$ (b) $6 \times 2 =$ ▢ $\times 4$

6 A pair of sunglasses costs $6 and a hat costs $7.
Wyatt bought 2 pairs of sunglasses and 3 hats.
He paid with a $100 bill.

(a) How much did he spend on sunglasses?

(b) How much did he spend on hats?

(c) How much did he spend in all?

(d) How much change did he get?

7 Each bag of 3 party masks costs $5.
Susma bought 24 party masks.

(a) How many bags did she buy?

(b) How much did she spend?

8 Maurice spent $15 on balloons.
There are 10 balloons in each bag.
He used 35 balloons at a party.

(a) How many balloons did he buy?
(b) How many balloons did he have left?

9 How much do 5 bags of party hats
and 9 bags of balloons cost?

10 10 lb of cherries cost $20.
Debra bought 5 lb of cherries.
How much did she spend?

11 Ella saved $3 a week for 10 weeks.
She wants to buy gifts that cost $5 each for her friends.
How many gifts can she buy?

12 1 table can seat 4 people.
What is the fewest number of
tables needed to seat 34 people?

13 Carter made a paper chain for the party.
He put 4 yellow strips between every red strip.
There are 8 red strips in the chain.
How many yellow strips are there?

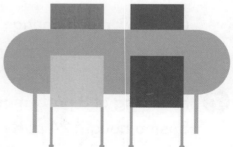

Exercise 9 • page 51

Chapter 10

Money

Think

Count the amount of money Mei, Alex, and Sofia have.

Alex's money

Sofia's money

Mei's money

How much more money do Mei and Sofia need so they have the same amount of money as Alex?

Learn

I have 1 dollar.

Alex has $ _____ .

25¢   30¢   40¢   50¢   60¢   65¢

I have 65 cents.

Sofia has ▢ ¢.

25¢   50¢   75¢   85¢   95¢   96¢   97¢   98¢   99¢   100¢

Mei has $▢.

I have 100¢ cents.
I have the same amount
of money as Alex.

There are 100 cents in 1 dollar.
100¢ = $1

$1 − 65¢ = ▢ ¢

100 − 65 = ?

Sofia needs ▢ ¢ more to have $1.

Make $1 with coins
in different ways!

Do

1 Find the missing amount of money.

(a)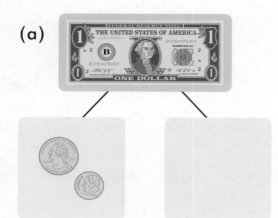

(b)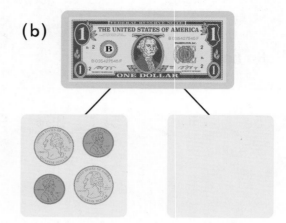

(c)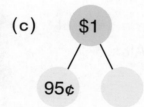

(d)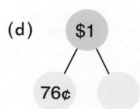

(e)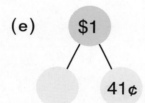

(f)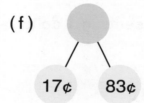

2 (a) $1 − 40¢ = ☐ ¢

(b) $1 − 4¢ = ☐ ¢

(c) $1 − 55¢ = ☐ ¢

(d) $1 − 23¢ = ☐ ¢

3 Emma buys a toy for 85¢.
She pays with a $1 bill.
How much change does she receive?

Exercise 1 • page 55

10-1 Making $1

Think

Dion bought a board game.
He paid with these bills and coins.

How much did he spend?

Learn

Count the dollars.

$10 $15 $16 $17

Count the cents.

25¢   35¢   45¢   50¢   51¢   52¢   53¢

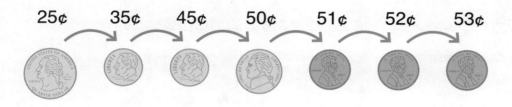

10, 15, 16, 17 dollars.
25, 35, 45, 50, 51, 52, 53 cents.
17 dollars and 53 cents.

He spent **$17.53**.

$17.53 is **seventeen dollars and fifty-three cents.**

The dot (.) separates the cents from the dollars.

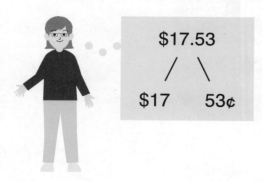

$17.53

$17   53¢

Do

1 Show the following amounts with bills and coins.

(a) 2 dollars and 70 cents

(b) $7.35

(c) $18

$15.00 is the same as $15.

(d) $15.00

(e) 80¢

$0.45 is the same as 45¢.
We write $0.45, not $.45.

(f) $0.45

(g) $5.40

We write $5.04, not $5.4,
for 5 dollars and 4 cents.

(h) $5.04

2 How much does each item cost?

(a) 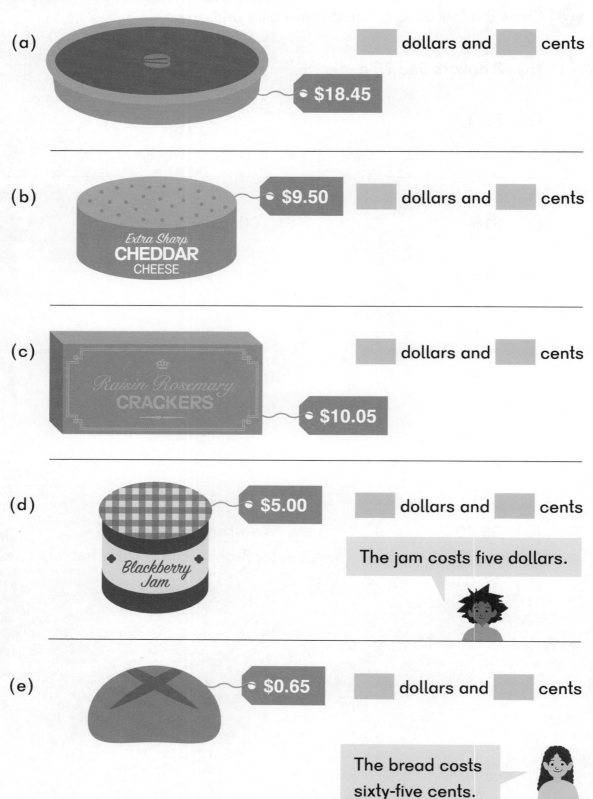 $18.45

　　　dollars and 　　cents

(b) $9.50　　dollars and 　　cents

(c) 　　dollars and 　　cents

$10.05

(d) $5.00　　dollars and 　　cents

The jam costs five dollars.

(e) $0.65　　dollars and 　　cents

The bread costs sixty-five cents.

3 Write the amount as $ ▯ . ▯ .

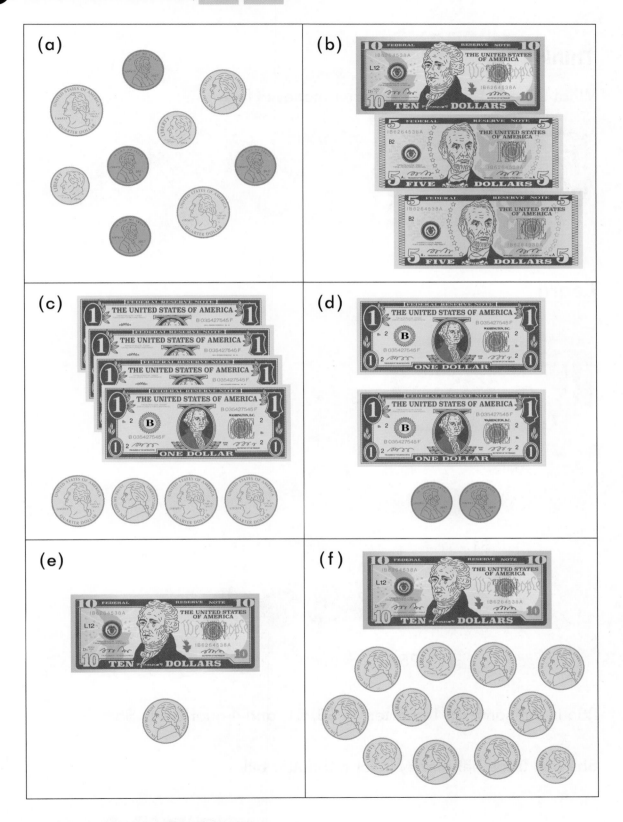

Lesson 3
Making Change

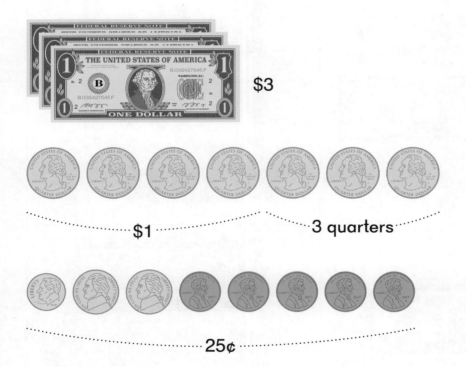

Think

What bill can Emma trade all her money in for?

Learn

$3

$1   3 quarters

25¢

25¢ is the same as 1 quarter. | $3, $1, and 4 quarters is $5.

She can trade her money in for a 5-dollar bill.

Do

1 Use bills and coins to make $5 in different ways.

I used bills for $2 and quarters for the rest.

4 quarters = 100¢

$5 = $5.00 = 500¢

8 quarters = 200¢ = $⬚

12 quarters = 300¢ = $⬚

$2 + $3 = $⬚

2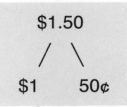

6 quarters = $⬚.⬚

$1.50

$1 ⟍ 50¢

3

3 quarters and 4 dimes = $ ▢ . ▢

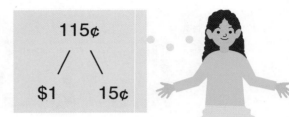

115¢
/ \
$1   15¢

4 Write the amount as $ ▢ . ▢ .

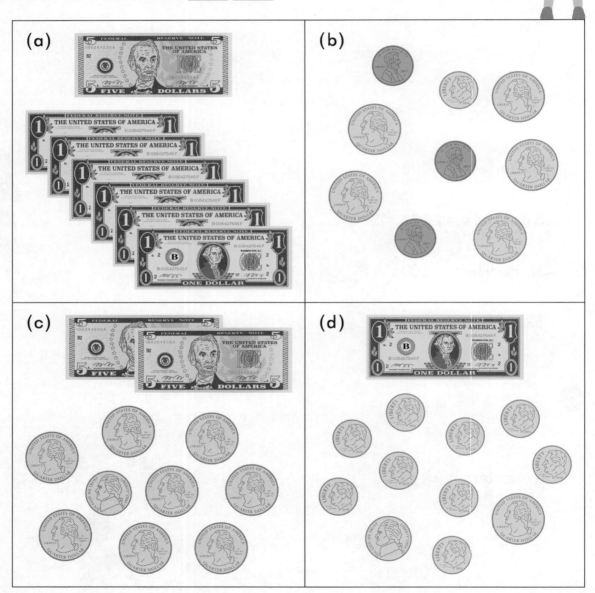

(a)

(b)

(c)

(d)

5 (a) 65¢ = $ [ ] . [ ]

(b) 100¢ = $ [ ] . [ ]

(c) 125¢ = $ [ ] . [ ]

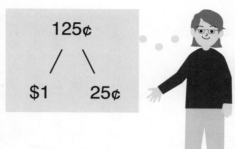

(d) 230¢ = $ [ ] . [ ]

(e) 503¢ = $ [ ] . [ ]

6 (a) $1.00 = [ ] ¢

(b) $2.09 = [ ] ¢

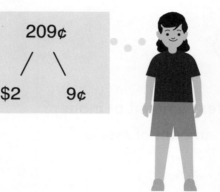

(c) $2.90 = [ ] ¢

(d) $0.45 = [ ] ¢

(e) $6 = [ ] ¢

7 Write the amount as both $ [ ] . [ ] and [ ] ¢.

(a) 30 dimes

(b) 5 quarters and 5 nickels

(c) 2 one-dollar bills, 6 quarters, and 4 pennies

(d) 5 pennies, 12 dimes, and 1 five-dollar bill

Exercise 3 · page 61

Think

Emma's money

Dion's money

Alex's money

Who has the greatest amount of money?

Who has the least amount of money?

Learn

Compare Emma's money and Dion's money.

Dollars	Cents	
7 •	27	Emma
4 •	27	Dion

$7 > $4

$7.27 $\bigcirc$ $4.27

_____ has more money than _____.

Compare Dion's money and Alex's money.

Dollars	Cents	
4 •	27	Dion
7 •	26	Alex

$4 $\bigcirc$ $7

$4.27 $\bigcirc$ $7.26

_____ has less money than _____.

Compare Alex's money and Emma's money.

Dollars	Cents	
7 •	26	Alex
7 •	27	Emma

26¢ $\bigcirc$ 27¢

$7.26 $\bigcirc$ $7.27

_____ has more money than _____.

_____ has the greatest amount of money.

_____ has the least amount of money.

Do

1 Which set has more money?

2 Which set has less money?

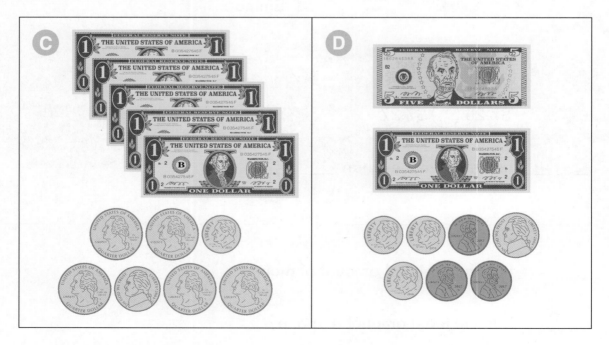

3 Which roll of tape is less expensive?

E $5.99   F $9.55

4 Which dip is more expensive?

G Guacamole $8.29   H Red Salsa $8.09

5 What sign, > or <, goes in the ◯?

(a) $8.99 ◯ $9.30   (b) $5.68 ◯ $5.90

(c) 75¢ ◯ $0.69   (d) $4 ◯ $0.40

(e) 103¢ ◯ $1.30   (f) $5 ◯ 63¢

6 Put the price tags in order from least expensive to most expensive.

(a) $3.20 $2.99 $3.02 $9.29

(b) $6.43 $6.34 $4.63 $3.46

(c) $0.99   63¢ $6 $6.03

Exercise 4 • page 65

1 (a) Write the amount of money in each set in words.

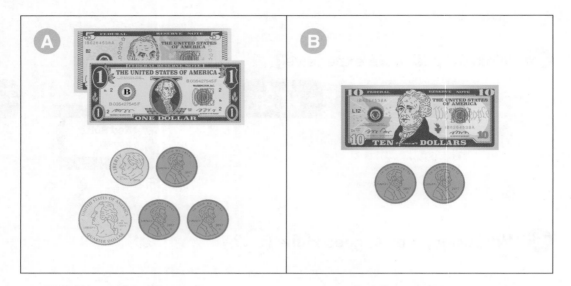

(b) Set _____ has more money than Set _____.

2 Write the amount of money in each set as $ ▢ . ▢ .

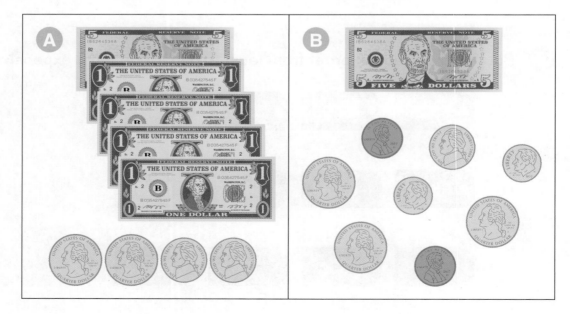

3 (a) 100¢ = $ ▢ . ▢

(b) 175¢ = $ ▢ . ▢

4 (a) $3.05 = ▢ ¢

(b) $0.43 = ▢ ¢

5 What sign, > or <, goes in the ◯?

(a) $1.99 ◯ $0.99

(b) $4.08 ◯ $4.80

(c) $3 ◯ 33¢

(d) $4 ◯ $3.44

6 Put the price tags in order from most expensive to least expensive.

(a) ● $8.30   ● $8.03   ● $9   ● $8.00

(b) ● $1.10   ● $10   ● $1.00   ● $0.10

7 Jason wants to buy a toothbrush that costs $1.00.
He has 68¢.
How much more money does he need?

8 Lily bought a roll of floss that cost $0.90.
She paid with a 1-dollar bill.
How much change did she receive?

Exercise 5 • page 69

Think

Mei bought a pair of scissors for $6.25 and a key chain for $3.40.
How much did she spend altogether?

Learn

Method 1

Add the dollars and cents separately.

$6 + $3 = $⬜

25¢ + 40¢ = ⬜¢

$6.25 + $3.40 = $⬜.⬜

Method 2

Add the dollars, then the cents.

$6.25 $\xrightarrow{+\ \$3}$ $⬜.⬜ $\xrightarrow{+\ 40¢}$ $⬜.⬜

She spent $_____.

Do

1 (a) Add $4.35 and $3.23.

$4.35 + $3.23 = $_____

(b) Add $3.20 and $5.25.

$3.20 $\xrightarrow{\text{+ \$5}}$ $ [ ] . [ ] $\xrightarrow{\text{+ 25¢}}$ $ [ ] . [ ]

$3.20 + $5.25 = $_____

2 Find the value.

(a) $4.55 + $3 = $ [ ] . [ ]

(b) $0.27 + $2 = $ [ ] . [ ]

(c) 30¢ + 15¢ = $ [ ] . [ ]

(d) $3.20 + 65¢ = $ [ ] . [ ]

(e) $0.55 + $6.05 = $ [ ] . [ ]

(f) $8.22 + $1.36 = $ [ ] . [ ]

3 (a) Add 1.75¢ and 25¢.

75 + 25 = 100

$1.75 + 25¢ = $ ▢

(b) Add $3.55 and $2.45.

$3.55 → **+ $2** → $ ▢ . ▢ → **+ 45¢** → $ ▢ . ▢

$3.55 + $2.45 = $ ▢

4 (a) Add 65¢ and 55¢.

60¢ + 40¢ = $1
5¢ + 15¢ = ...

65 + 55
35   20

65¢ + 55¢ = $ ▢ . ▢

(b) Add $4.85 and $2.50.

$4.85 $\xrightarrow{\ +\ \$2\ }$ $6.85 $\xrightarrow{\ +\ 15¢\ }$ $7 $\xrightarrow{\ +\ 35¢\ }$ $▢ . ▢

$4.85 + $2.50 = $▢ . ▢

5 (a) 35¢ + 65¢ = $▢ . ▢ $3.35 + 65¢ = $▢ . ▢

(b) $3.85 + $0.15 = $▢ . ▢ $3.85 + $0.20 = $▢ . ▢

(c) $7.90 + $1.25 = $▢ . ▢ $7.90 + $1.85¢ = $▢ . ▢

6 Find the value.

(a) $2.07 + $7.00   (b) $5.35 + $2.05

(c) $4.53 + $0.35   (d) $3.60 + $0.40

(e) $1.75 + $0.50   (f) $6.80 + $2.50

(g) $1.55 + $4.55   (h) $0.85 + $7.50

7 What is the total cost of the 3 fruits?

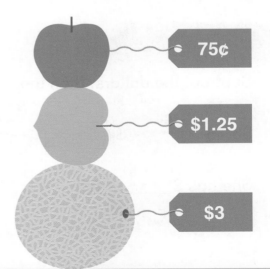

75¢

$1.25

$3

Exercise 6 • page 73

Think

Sofia has $6.75.

She buys a burrito for $4.50.

How much money does she have left?

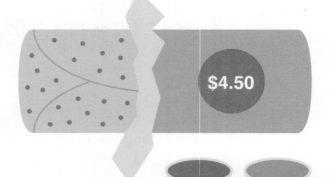

Learn

Method 1

Subtract the dollars and cents separately.

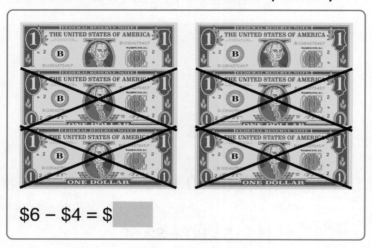

$6 − $4 = $ [____]

75¢ − 50¢ = [____] ¢

$6.75 − $4.50 = $ [____] . [____]

Method 2

Subtract the dollars, then the cents.

$6.75 —$4→ $ [____] . [____] —50¢→ $ [____] . [____]

She has $_____ left.

Do

1 (a) Subtract $3.40 from $5.65.

$5.65 − $3.40 = $_____

(b) Subtract $2.50 from $8.70.

$8.70 $\xrightarrow{-\$2}$ $ [ ] . [ ] $\xrightarrow{-50¢}$ $ [ ] . [ ]

$8.70 − $2.50 = $_____

2 (a) $4.55 − $3 = $ [ ] . [ ]   (b) $8.27 − $2 = $ [ ] . [ ]

(c) 80¢ − 15¢ = $ [ ] . [ ]   (d) $3.70 − 65¢ = $ [ ] . [ ]

(e) $4.75 − $0.55 = $ [ ] . [ ]   (f) $8.96 − $1.32 = $ [ ] . [ ]

3 (a) Subtract 40¢ from $3.

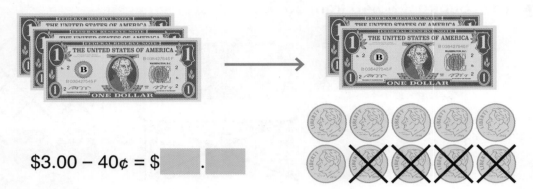

$3.00 − 40¢ = $ ⬜.⬜

(b) Subtract $2.75 from $5.

$5.00 $\xrightarrow{-\$2}$ $ ⬜.⬜ $\xrightarrow{-75¢}$ $ ⬜.⬜

$5.00 − $2.75 = $ ⬜.⬜

4 (a) Subtract 80¢ from $4.20.

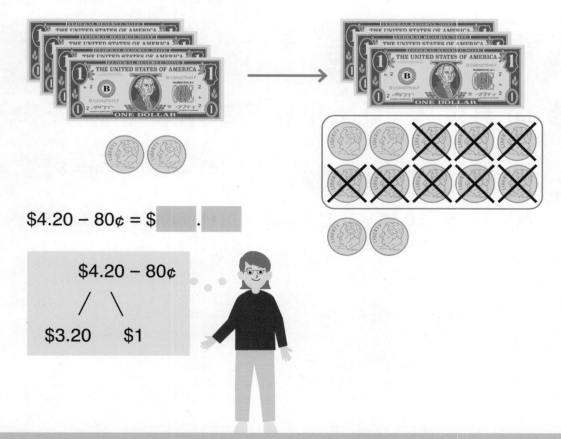

$4.20 − 80¢ = $ ⬜.⬜

$4.20 − 80¢

/ \

$3.20 $1

(b) Subtract $2.80 from $4.20.

$4.20 $\xrightarrow{-\$2}$ $2.20 $\xrightarrow{-80¢}$ \$ [ ] . [ ]

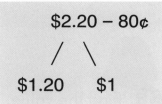

$2.20 – 80¢

$1.20 $1

$4.20 – $2.80 = \$ [ ] . [ ]

5 (a) $1 – 65¢ = \$ [ ] . [ ] $6 – 65¢ = \$ [ ] . [ ]

(b) $6 – $3.65 = \$ [ ] . [ ] $6.20 – $3.65 = \$ [ ] . [ ]

(c) $8 – 45¢ = \$ [ ] . [ ] $8.05 – $4.45 = \$ [ ] . [ ]

6 Find the value.

(a) $5.95 – $4.00   (b) $4.75 – $0.50

(c) $9.85 – $3.40   (d) $7.99 – $2.11

(e) $2.00 – $0.75   (f) $6.00 – $1.80

(g) $3.10 – $0.45   (h) $8.50 – $4.85

7 Alex has $7.
He buys a pear for 65¢ and some peanuts for $3.25.
How much money does he have left?

Exercise 7 • page 77

1 Find the value.

(a) 35¢ + 65¢

(b) $6.20 + 35¢

(c) $2.87 + $4

(d) $5.06 + $4.10

(e) $2.08 + $1.09

(f) 65¢ + 55¢

(g) 8¢ + $1.92

(h) $0.90 + $0.25

(i) $3.50 + $2.75

(j) $5.35 + $1.80

2 Franco saved $5.40 this week and $3.85 last week.
How much did he save in the two weeks altogether?

$5.40 ········· $3.85

| this week | last week |

3 Misha buys a notebook that costs $2.75.
She pays for it with a $5 bill.
How much change will she get back?

$5

| notebook | change |

$2.75

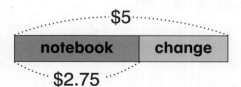

• $2.75

NOTE BOOK

198 pages / 8.5" × 11"
Recycled Materials

4 Find the value.

(a) 95¢ – 60¢

(b) $3.52 – $2

(c) $8.75 – 50¢

(d) $6.40 – $1.20

(e) $7.45 – $2.15

(f) $4 – 90¢

(g) $2.00 – $1.95

(h) $7.20 – $1.75

(i) $4.10 – $2.40

(j) $7.00 – $5.99

5 Jody wants to buy a plant that costs $5.45 and plant food that costs $3.40. He has $8.

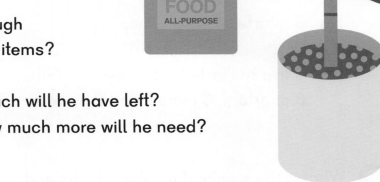

(a) Does he have enough money to buy both items?

(b) If he does, how much will he have left? If he does not, how much more will he need?

6 Katie and Onawa saved $9.85 altogether. Katie saved $5.50.

(a) How much did Onowa save?

(b) How much more did Katie save than Onawa?

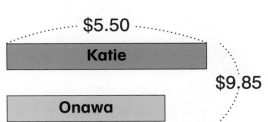

$5.50

Katie

Onawa

$9.85

7 What sign, >, <, or =, goes in the ◯?

(a) 65¢ ◯ $6.50

(b) $5 ◯ 96¢

(c) $8.60 ◯ 806¢

(d) $7 ◯ $0.70

(e) $6.40 + 72¢ ◯ $6.72 + 40¢

(f) $6 + 55¢ ◯ $7 – $0.55

(g) $1 – $0.85 ◯ $9 – $8.85

8 Write the amount as $ ▢ . ▢ .

(a) 2 five-dollar bills and 8 pennies

(b) 1 five-dollar bill and 6 nickels

(c) 3 quarters and 9 dimes

(d) 3 five-dollar bills, 3 one-dollar bills,
3 quarters, 3 dimes, and 3 nickels

9 What is the smallest number of bills and coins
needed to make $9.40 exactly?

10 Paula has 7 coins.
The 7 coins make $1.35.
What are the coins?

Exercise 8 • page 81

10-8 Practice B

Chapter 11

Fractions

Think

How can we cut the square flatbread into 2 equal parts?

How can we cut the flatbread into 4 equal parts?

How big is each part compared to the whole piece of flatbread?

How can we write the answer as a number?

Learn

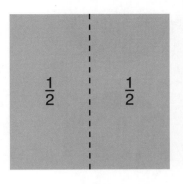

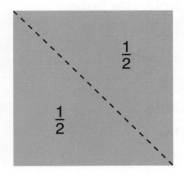

Fractions are numbers that count equally divided parts of the whole.

When we divide a shape into 2 equal parts, each part is **one-half** of the whole.
We write one-half as $\frac{1}{2}$.
$\frac{1}{2}$ means 1 out of 2 equally divided parts.

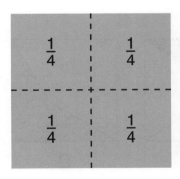

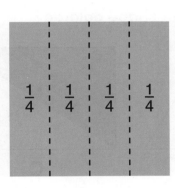

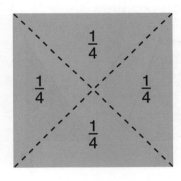

When we divide a shape into 4 equal parts, each part is **one-fourth** of the whole.
We write one-fourth as $\frac{1}{4}$.
$\frac{1}{4}$ means 1 out of 4 equally divided parts.

One-fourth is also called **one-quarter**.

Do

1 (a) Fold and cut a paper circle into halves.

How many halves make 1 whole?

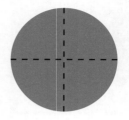

(b) Fold and cut a paper circle
the same size into fourths.

How many fourths make 1 whole?

(c) How many fourths make 1 half?

(d) Which is bigger, $\frac{1}{2}$ of the circle or $\frac{1}{4}$ of the circle?

2 Which pictures show $\frac{1}{2}$ of the shape colored?

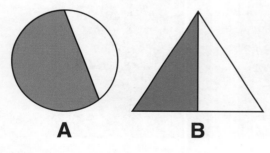
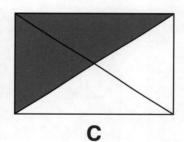
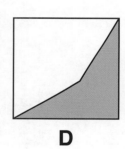

A   **B**   **C**   **D**

3 Which pictures show $\frac{1}{4}$ of the shape colored?

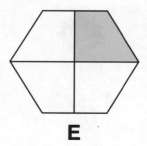
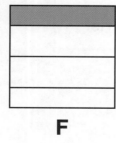
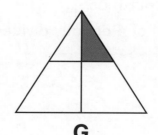
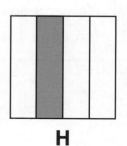

E   **F**   **G**   **H**

Exercise 1 • page 85

Think

How can we cut the brownies into 8 equal parts?

How big is each part compared to the whole?

Learn

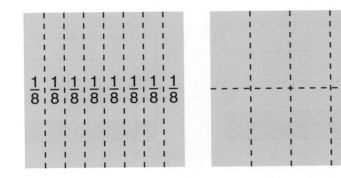

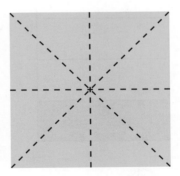

When we divide a shape into 8 equal parts, each part is **one-eighth** of the whole.
We write one-eighth as $\frac{1}{8}$.
$\frac{1}{8}$ means 1 out of 8 equally divided parts.

How many eighths make 1 whole?

Do

 (a) Fold a paper strip into 3 equal parts.

What fraction of the paper strip is one part?

(b) Fold the same paper strip into 6 equal parts.

What fraction of the paper strip is one part?

2 What fraction of each rectangle is colored?

(a) 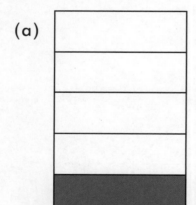   (b)    (c)

The wholes are the same size,
but the size of the parts is different.

3 What fraction of each circle is colored?

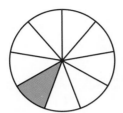 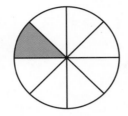 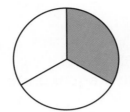 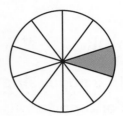

4 What fraction of each shape is colored?

(a)
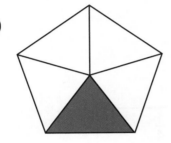

(b)
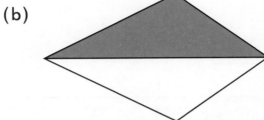

(c)
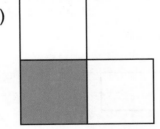

(d)
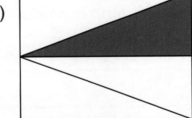

(e)
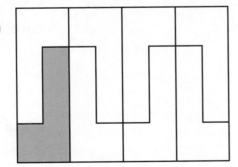

(f)
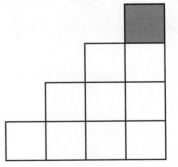

Exercise 2 • page 87

Think

Fold a paper strip into 4 equal parts.
Color 3 parts.

What fraction of the paper strip is colored?

Learn

$\frac{1}{4}$	$\frac{1}{4}$	$\frac{1}{4}$	$\frac{1}{4}$

1 out of 4 equal parts is colored.
$\frac{1}{4}$ of the paper strip is colored.

$\frac{1}{4}$	$\frac{1}{4}$	$\frac{1}{4}$	$\frac{1}{4}$

3 out of 4 equal parts are colored.
3 fourths of the paper strip are colored.
We write three-fourths as $\frac{3}{4}$.

There are ▢ one-fourths in $\frac{3}{4}$.

is also $\frac{3}{4}$ colored.

Do

1 How many one-fifths are in 4 fifths?

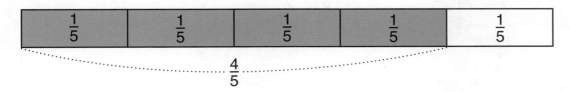

There are ▢ one-fifths in $\frac{4}{5}$.

2 How many one-eighths are in 5 eighths?

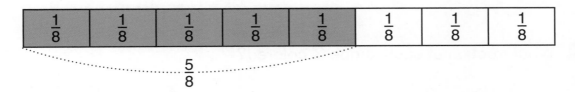

There are ▢ one-eighths in $\frac{5}{8}$.

3 (a)

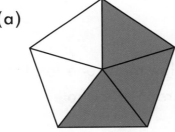

▢ out of the ▢ equal parts are colored.

$\frac{3}{5}$ of the shape is colored.

(b)

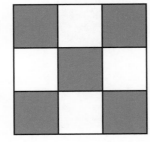

▢ out of the ▢ equal parts are colored.

▢ of the shape is colored.

4 What fraction of each circle is colored?

(a)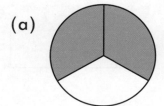

(b)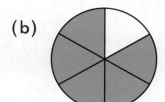

(c)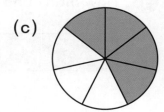

(d)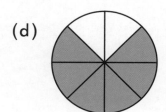

(e)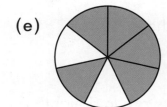

(f)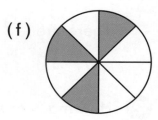

5 What fraction of each shape is colored?

(a)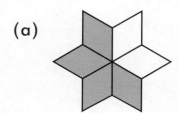

(b)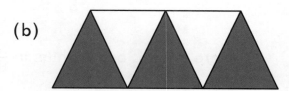

6 (a) How many one-thirds are in one whole?

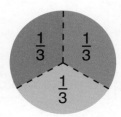

(b) How many one-fourths are in one whole?

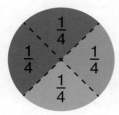

(c) How many one-ninths are in one whole?

Exercise 3 • page 91

11-3 Writing Fractions

Lesson 4
Fractions that Make 1 Whole

④

Think

This is a whole chocolate bar.

Alex ate part of the chocolate bar.
This is how much of the chocolate bar that is left.

(a)   What fraction of the chocolate bar did he eat?

(b)   What fraction of the chocolate bar is left?

Learn

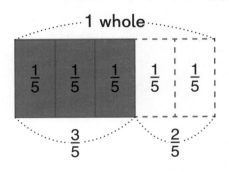

1 whole

$\frac{1}{5}$ $\frac{1}{5}$ $\frac{1}{5}$ $\frac{1}{5}$ $\frac{1}{5}$

$\frac{3}{5}$ $\frac{2}{5}$

5 fifths is 1 whole.

(a)   He ate ▮ of the chocolate bar.

$\frac{3}{5}$ and $\frac{2}{5}$ make 1 whole.

(b)   ▮ of the chocolate bar is left.

Do

1 (a) What fraction of the rectangle is purple?

(b) What fraction of the rectangle is green?

(c) $\frac{7}{10}$ and [ ] make 1 whole.

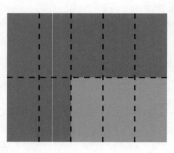

2 (a)

$\frac{3}{4}$ and $\frac{1}{4}$ make [ ] whole.

(b)

$\frac{3}{5}$ and [ ] make 1 whole.

(c)

1 whole is $\frac{3}{6}$ and [ ].

(d)

[ ] and $\frac{3}{8}$ make 1 whole.

3 What fraction will make 1 whole with each?

(a) $\frac{2}{3}$ (b) $\frac{1}{2}$ (c) $\frac{2}{9}$

(d) $\frac{4}{5}$ (e) $\frac{3}{7}$ (f) $\frac{8}{10}$

Exercise 4 · page 95

Think

Use 3 paper strips of the same length.
Fold one into halves, one into thirds, and one into fourths.

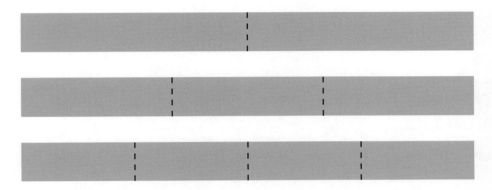

(a) Which fraction is the largest, $\frac{1}{2}$, $\frac{1}{3}$, or $\frac{1}{4}$?

(b) Which fraction is the smallest, $\frac{1}{2}$, $\frac{1}{3}$, or $\frac{1}{4}$?

Learn

Compare $\frac{1}{2}$ and $\frac{1}{3}$.

$\frac{1}{2}$ is larger than $\frac{1}{3}$.

is smaller than .

Compare $\frac{1}{2}$ and $\frac{1}{4}$.

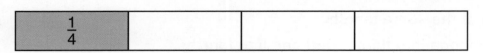

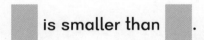

$\frac{1}{2}$ is larger than $\frac{1}{4}$.

 is smaller than .

Compare $\frac{1}{3}$ and $\frac{1}{4}$.

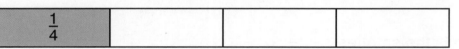

 is larger than .

 is smaller than .

(a) Of $\frac{1}{2}$, $\frac{1}{3}$, and $\frac{1}{4}$, the largest fraction is .

(b) Of $\frac{1}{2}$, $\frac{1}{3}$, and $\frac{1}{4}$, the smallest fraction is .

(c) Arrange the fractions $\frac{1}{2}$, $\frac{1}{3}$, and $\frac{1}{4}$, in order. Begin with the smallest.

When the whole is divided into more equal parts, the size of each part is smaller.

Do

1 Which is larger, $\frac{1}{3}$ or $\frac{1}{5}$?

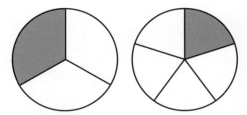

There are fewer parts
in the whole for thirds
than for fifths,
so each part is larger.

2 Which is smaller, $\frac{1}{4}$ or $\frac{1}{8}$?

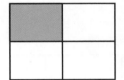 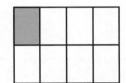

There are more parts
in the whole for eighths
than for fourths,
so each part is smaller.

3 (a) Which is larger, $\frac{1}{7}$ or $\frac{1}{5}$?

   (b) Which is smaller, $\frac{1}{6}$ or $\frac{1}{9}$?

4 Arrange the fractions in order.
Begin with the smallest.

(a) $\boxed{\frac{1}{2}}$ $\boxed{\frac{1}{8}}$ $\boxed{\frac{1}{5}}$

(b) $\boxed{\frac{1}{7}}$ $\boxed{\frac{1}{9}}$ $\boxed{\frac{1}{4}}$

(c) $\boxed{\frac{1}{6}}$ $\boxed{\frac{1}{10}}$ $\boxed{\frac{1}{3}}$

Exercise 5 • page 97

1 What fraction of each circle is colored?

(a)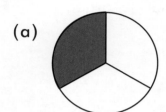

(b)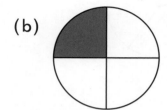

(c)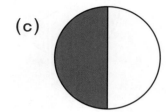

2 What fraction of each shape is colored?

(a)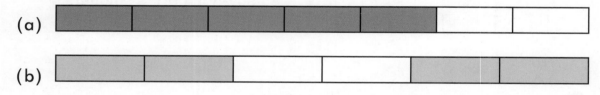

(b)

(c)

3 (a)

$\frac{4}{9}$ and ▢ make 1 whole.

(b)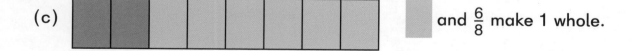

$\frac{2}{5}$ and ▢ make 1 whole.

(c) ▢ and $\frac{6}{8}$ make 1 whole.

4 Some of 1 whole paper strip was torn off.
Each part shown below is $\frac{1}{6}$ of a whole.
How many parts were torn off?

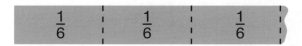

5 Arrange the fractions in order. Begin with the smallest.

(a) $\boxed{\dfrac{1}{5}}$ $\boxed{\dfrac{1}{7}}$ $\boxed{\dfrac{1}{10}}$

(b) $\boxed{\dfrac{1}{6}}$ $\boxed{\dfrac{1}{8}}$ $\boxed{\dfrac{1}{9}}$

6 Mary, Chapa, and Diego
each ate one piece of pie.
What fraction of the pie
did they eat altogether?

7 Marissa made some lasagna.
She cut it into 8 pieces and ate 3 pieces.
What fraction of the lasagna was left?

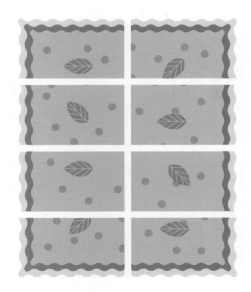

8 Fang ate $\frac{1}{6}$ of a pizza.
James ate $\frac{1}{4}$ of the same pizza.
Who ate more pizza?

Exercise 6 • page 101

① Find the value.

(a) 507 + 65   (b) 152 + 73   (c) 688 + 55

(d) 952 − 91   (e) 327 + 286   (f) 703 − 146

(g) 485 + 8   (h) 499 + 98   (i) 730 − 7

(j) 600 − 97   (k) 400 − 135   (l) 390 − 57

② Which of the following are good estimates for the length of a bathtub?

2 ft   2 m   6 ft   6 m

③ Which of the following are good estimates for the weight of a cat?

7 lb   30 lb   3 kg   15 kg

④ (a) $\frac{7}{10}$ and ▢ make 1 whole.

(b) There are ▢ one-sevenths in $\frac{4}{7}$.

⑤ Sharon has 2 one-dollar bills, 9 quarters, 7 dimes, 6 nickels, and 5 pennies.
Write the amount of money as both $ ▢ . ▢ and ▢ ¢.

6 Find the value.

   (a) 2 × 7

   (b) 6 × 4

   (c) 8 × 5

   (d) 3 × 6

   (e) 4 × 10

   (f) 4 × 4

   (g) 18 ÷ 2

   (h) 27 ÷ 3

   (i) 50 ÷ 5

   (j) 28 ÷ 4

   (k) 36 ÷ 4

   (l) 60 ÷ 10

7 Trevor and 4 friends are sharing 45 grapes equally.
How many grapes will each child get?

8 There are 8 tricycles.
How many wheels are there?

9 Angela walked 526 m from her house to the store.
Then she walked 397 m from the store to the library.
How far did she walk in all?

10 A picture book weighs 375 g.
A coloring book weighs 280 g.

   (a) How much less does the coloring book weigh than the picture book?

   (b) How much do they weigh together?

11 What sign, >, <, or =, goes in the $\bigcirc$?

(a) $40 + 700 + 1 \bigcirc 400 + 10 + 7$ (b) $6 \times 4 \bigcirc 5 \times 4 + 3$

(c) $584 + 392 \bigcirc 382 + 594$ (d) $3 \times 7 \bigcirc 9 \times 3$

(e) $803 + 195 \bigcirc 506 - 397$ (f) $1 \text{ cm} \bigcirc 1 \text{ in}$

(g) $200 + 40 + 6 \bigcirc 254 - 8$ (h) $\$503 \bigcirc 530¢$

12 Ms. Gonzalez has 4 baskets with 10 apples in each basket.
She wants to put the apples equally into 5 bags.
How many apples should she put in each bag?

13 Yara had $300.
She spent $150 on a jacket and $97 on a pair of shoes.
How much money does she have left?

14 Carson buys a drink that costs 75¢ and a sandwich that costs $3.35.
He pays with a 5-dollar bill.
How much change does he get?

Exercise 7 • page 105

Chapter 12

Time

Our friends are having fun on Sports Day.
What time are they doing each activity?

Think

Mei's math class started at 10:00.
What time is it now?

Learn

The longer hand is the **minute hand**.
The shorter hand is the **hour hand**.

It is five minutes after ten.
It is ten oh five.

It is ten fifteen.

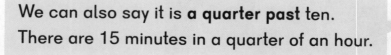

We can also say it is **a quarter past** ten.
There are 15 minutes in a quarter of an hour.

It is ten thirty.

We can also say it is **half past** ten. The hour hand is halfway between 10 and 11. There are 30 minutes in half of an hour.

It is ten forty-five.

We can also say it is a **quarter to eleven**.

It is ten fifty-three.

To count the minutes, count by fives, then add 3. Look at the hour hand to see which hour it is.

It is 7 minutes to eleven.

Do

1 (a) Count by fives to 60.

(b) How many minutes are there in one hour?

(c) How many 5-minute intervals are there from 12:00 to 1:00?

2 (a)

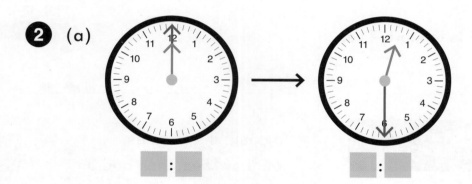

It is ▢ minutes past 12.

(b)

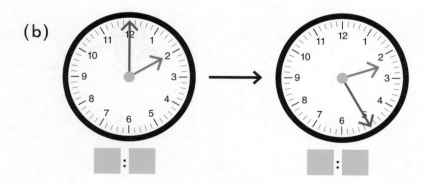

It is ▢ minutes past ▢ .

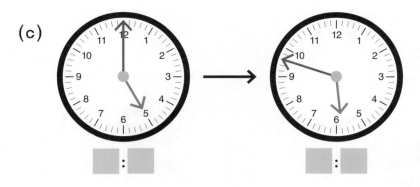

(c)

[ ] : [ ]   [ ] : [ ]

It is [ ] minutes past [ ].

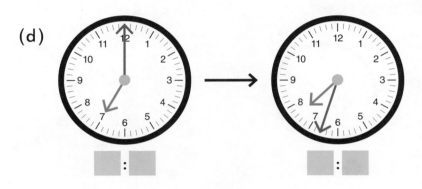

(d)

[ ] : [ ]   [ ] : [ ]

It is [ ] minutes past [ ].

3 How many minutes is it before the hour?

(a) [ ] minutes to 2.

(b) [ ] minutes to [ ].

(c) [ ] minutes to [ ].

4 What time is it?

5 How long was Emma's swim class?

Exercise 1 • page 111

12-1 Telling Time

Think

This is Alex's afternoon schedule.

Gym 12:10  Science 1:10  Snack 1:55  Music 2:10

How much time is there between the start of the first class or activity and the start of the second one for each of the following?

(a) Gym and Science   (b) Gym and Music

(c) Science and Snack   (d) Snack and Music

Learn

(a) Gym 12:10  [ ] hour later Science 1:10

Between 12:10 and 1:10, the minute hand moves all the way around the clock once.

(b)   Gym 12:10   Music 2:10

   ☐ hours later   

There are 2 one-hour intervals from 12:10 to 2:10.

(c)   Science 1:10   Snack 1:55

   ☐ minutes later   

There are 9 five-minute intervals from 1:10 to 1:55. $9 \times 5 = ?$

(d)   Snack 1:55   Music 2:10

   ☐ minutes later   

There are 3 five-minute intervals from 1:55 to 2:10.

Do

 How long does each activity last?

(a)

TV show

(b)

Baseball game

(c)

Music lesson

(d)

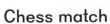

Chess match

(a)

What time will it
be in 4 hours?

(b)

What time was it
3 hours ago?

3 **(a)**

What time will it
be in 30 minutes?

(b)

What time was it
30 minutes ago?

(c)

What time will it
be in 15 minutes?

(d)

What time was it
15 minutes ago?

4 Alex's English class ended at 11:30.
The class was 45 minutes long.
What time did the class start?

Exercise 2 • page 115

12-2 Time Intervals

Think

The clocks show what time Sofia woke up and went to bed on Saturday.

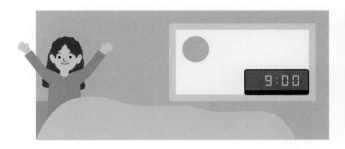 

What is the same about these two times?
What is different about these two times?

Learn

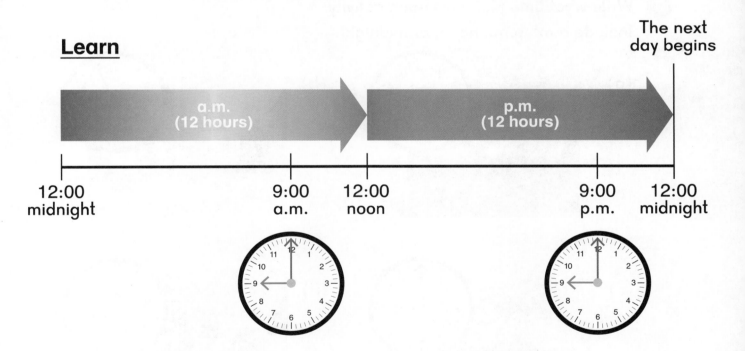

There are 24 hours in the day.

[   ] hours are in the a.m. and [   ] hours are in the p.m.
9:00 in the morning is 9:00 a.m. and 9:00 in the evening is 9:00 p.m.

<u>Do</u>

1 Write what time you usually do these activities.
Include a.m. or p.m.

    (a) Wake up.

    (b) Eat breakfast.

    (c) Leave for school.

    (d) Eat lunch.

    (e) Leave school.

    (f) Eat dinner.

    (g) Do your homework.

    (h) Go to bed.

2 Write what time Mei does each activity.
Include a.m., p.m., noon, or midnight.

(a)

(b)

(c)

(d)

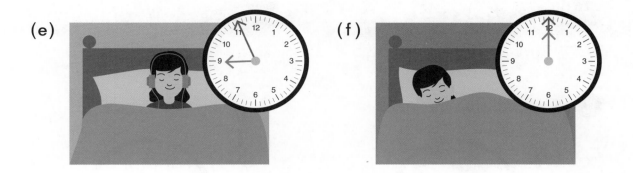

(e)

(f)

3 The clocks show when Dion's music class begins and ends.

Begin   End

(a) Write the start and end times. Include a.m. or p.m.

(b) How long is his music class?

4 The clocks show when Sofia's baseball game begins and ends.

Begin   End

10:10 AM   1:10 PM

How long was her game?

5 A tour began at 11:00 a.m. and lasted 5 hours. What time did it end?

Exercise 3 · page 121

1 Say and write the time.

(a)

(b)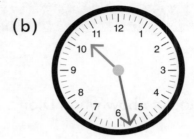

(c)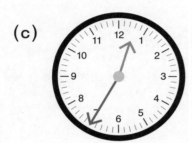

(d)

2 What time will it be when it is:

(a) 20 minutes after 1:30 p.m.

(b) 8 hours after 11:15 a.m.

(c) 35 minutes after 8:40 a.m.

(d) 4 hours before noon

(e) 4 hours after midnight

(f) Half an hour before 12:20 a.m.

3 A football game began at 6:30 p.m. and ended at 9:30 p.m. How long was the football game?

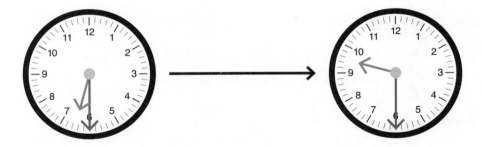

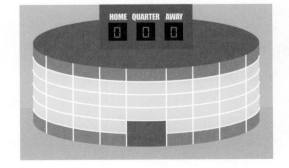

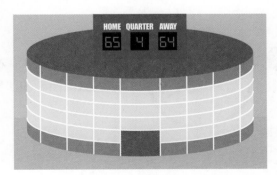

4 Pedro's band practice begins at 3:40 p.m. and ends at 4:35 p.m. How long is his band practice?

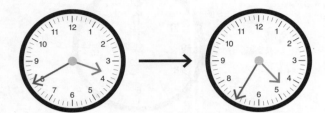

5  Sarah's computer class begins at 10:30 a.m. and lasts 40 minutes.
What time does her computer class end?

6  A concert began at 5:35 p.m. and lasted 4 hours.
What time did the concert end?

7  A 45-minute show ended at 12:15 p.m.
What time did the show start?

8  A 2-hour soccer match ended at 3:20 p.m.
What time did the match begin?

Exercise 4 • page 125

12-4 Practice

Chapter 13

Capacity

Think

Which pitcher can hold more water?

Learn

Fill both containers with water.
Then compare the amount of water.

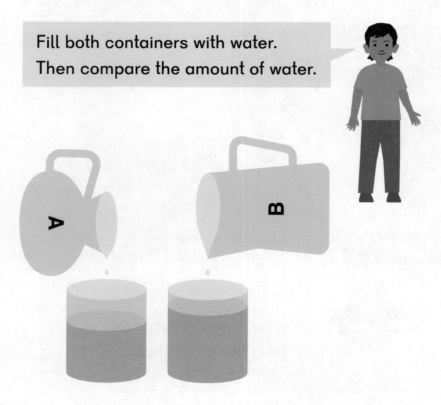

Pitcher _____ can hold more water than Pitcher _____.

The **capacity** of a container is the maximum amount of liquid it can hold. Pitcher B has a greater capacity than Pitcher A.

We can compare the capacity of containers by using equal units.

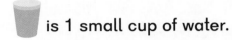 is 1 small cup of water.

How many of these cups of water can each container hold?

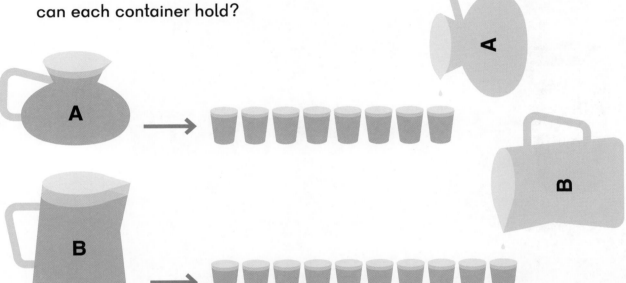

Pitcher A can hold ▢ cups of water.

Pitcher B can hold ▢ cups of water.

Pitcher B can hold ▢ more cups of water than Pitcher A.

Do

1 Use 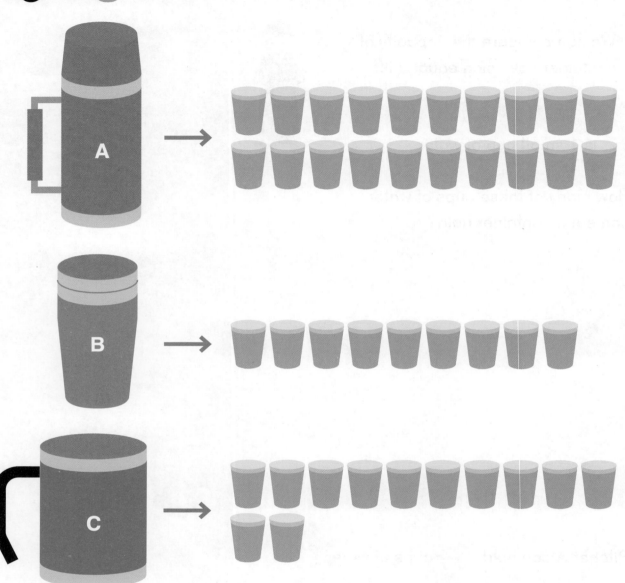 as 1 unit.

(a) Which thermos has the greatest capacity?

(b) Which thermos has the least capacity?

(c) Thermos C can hold ⬚ more units of water than Thermos B, and ⬚ fewer units of water than Thermos A.

2 This pitcher can hold the same amount of water as 7 glasses or 5 mugs.

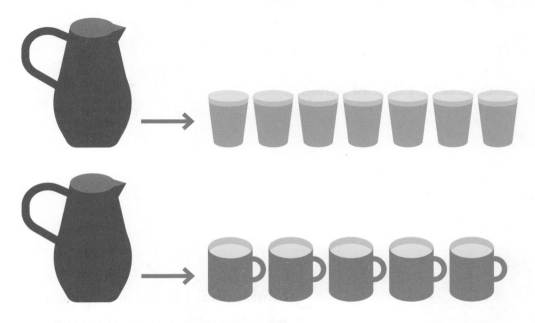

Which has a greater capacity, the mug or the glass?

3

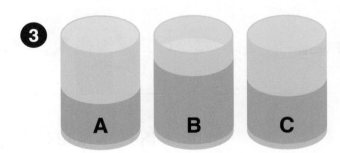

All 3 glasses have the same capacity, but are filled with different amounts of juice.

(a) Glass _____ has the most juice.

(b) Glass _____ is about half full.

(c) Glass _____ is less than half full.

Exercise 1 • page 129

Think

This container is filled with 1 liter of water.

I think about 8 small cups can be filled with 1 liter of water.

Estimate and then find out how many small cups can be filled with 1 liter of water.

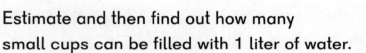

I think the tub holds about 5 liter of water.

Estimate and then find out how many liters of water a tub can hold.

Learn

The **liter** is a unit of capacity.
We write **L** for liter.

1 L of water can fill a little more than ⬜ of these cups.

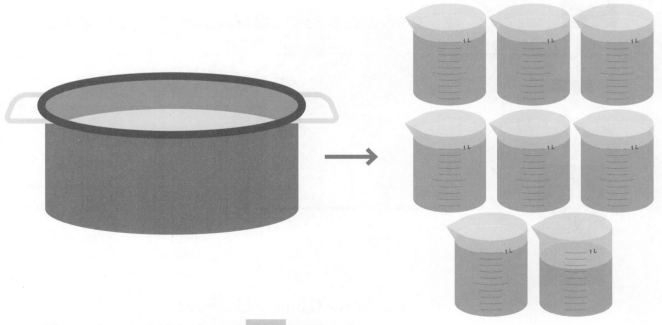

This tub can hold almost ⬜ L of water.

It has a capacity of about ⬜ L.

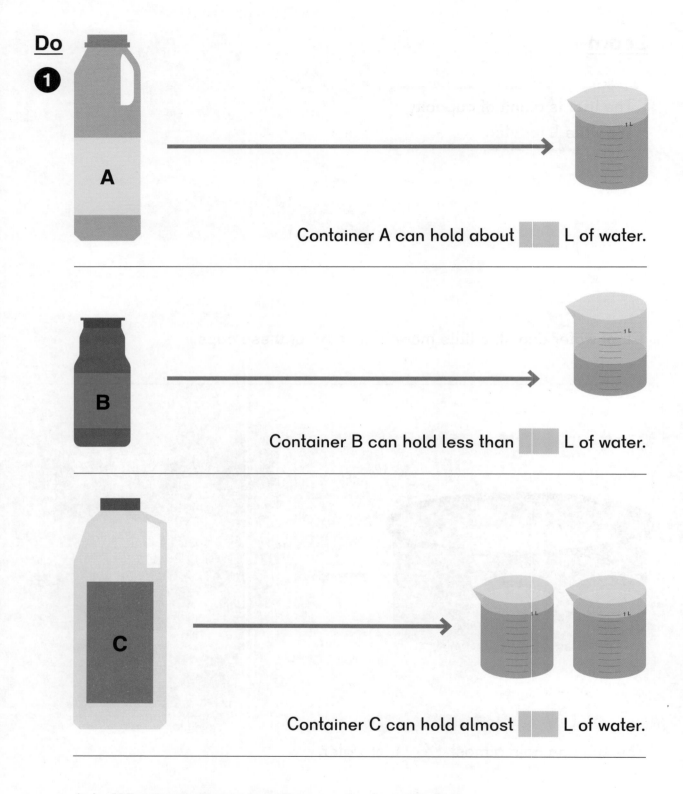

Container A can hold about ___ L of water.

Container B can hold less than ___ L of water.

Container C can hold almost ___ L of water.

(a) Which container has the greatest capacity?

(b) Which container has the least capacity?

2 (a)

The pot can hold ▢ L of water.

(b)

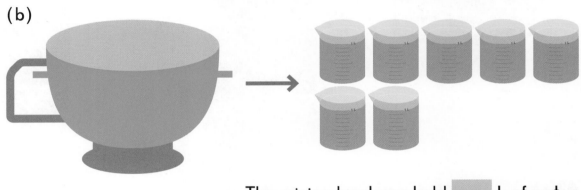

The mixing bowl can hold ▢ L of water.

(c) Which container has a greater capacity?

(d) How much greater is its capacity?

3 Estimate the capacity in liters of some containers.
Then measure their capacity in liters by pouring
the water into 1-liter containers.

4 There are other units of capacity,
such as gallons and quarts.
1 quart is just a little more than 1 liter.
There are 4 quarts in 1 gallon.

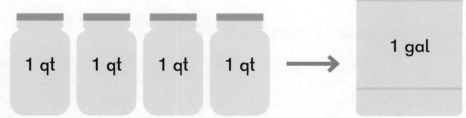

(a) ⬜ quarts are in 4 gallons.

(b) ⬜ quarts are in 8 gallons.

(c) 20 quarts are in ⬜ gallons.

Exercise 2 • page 133

13-2 Units of Capacity

1 An art teacher bought 12 gallons of paint.
After the students did a painting project,
she had 4 gallons of paint left.
How much paint did they use for the project?

2 Fish tank A has a capacity of 62 L of water.
Fish tank B has a capacity of 56 L of water.

(a) Which tank can hold more water?

(b) How much more?

3 The table shows the amount of water each child drank in 2 weeks.

Amelia	15 L
Evan	23 L
Hailey	18 L

(a) Who drank the greatest amount of water?

(b) Who drank the least amount of water?

(c) How much more water did Evan drink than Amelia?

(d) How much less water did Hailey drink than Evan?

4 A bucket can hold 10 L of water.
Isaac poured 5 buckets of water in an empty tank.
How much water is in the tank?

5 Violet buys 24 L of bottled water.
The water comes in jugs that hold 3 L of water.
How many jugs does she buy?

6 Cups are another unit of measure, often used in cooking.
There are 4 cups in 1 quart.

(a) Malik bought 3 quarts of cooking oil.
How many cups of oil did he buy?

(b) How many 1-quart jars are needed for 8 cups of jam?

7 1 L of water was poured into each of these containers.
They each have the same amount of water.
Explain why the level of water is different in each.

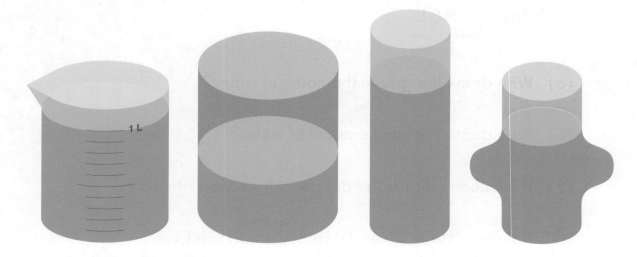

Exercise 3 • page 137

13-3 Practice

Chapter 14

Graphs

Out of chocolate, vanilla, or strawberry ice cream, which flavor do you like the best? Pick one.

Strawberry!

Chocolate!

Ice Cream Flavor	Tally
Chocolate	~~||||~~ ////
Vanilla	~~||||~~ /
Strawberry	////

~~||||~~ stands for 5.

What other things can you ask your friends about to make a tally chart?

Think

Emma recorded the number of items sold at the school store this week.
She showed the information in a **picture graph**.

Items Sold at the School Store this Week			
● ● ● ● ● ●	● ● ●	● ● ● ●	● ● ● ● ●
Pens	Erasers	Notebooks	Pencils

Each ● stands for 3 items.

What can you tell
from the graph?

Learn

_____ were sold the most.

_____ were sold the least.

I can see which item was sold the most and which was sold the least.

How many pens were sold?

$6 \times 3 = $

□ pens were sold.

I can find how many of each item was sold.

How many more pens were sold than erasers?

$3 \times 3 = $

□ more pens were sold than erasers.

I can compare how many of each item was sold.

How many items were sold in all?

$18 + 9 + 12 + 15 = $

□ items were sold in all.

I can find how many items were sold in all.

Do

1 This picture graph shows the number of people who attended the school art show this week.

School Art Show Attendance				
				■
			■	■
■		■	■	■
■	■	■	■	■
■	■	■	■	■
■	■	■	■	■
Monday	Tuesday	Wednesday	Thursday	Friday

Each ■ stands for 5 people.

(a) How many people went to the art show on Thursday?

(b) Which day had the highest attendance?

(c) Which day had the lowest attendance?

(d) Which 2 days had the same attendance?

(e) How many more people attended the show on Friday than on Monday?

(f) How many fewer people attended the show on Tuesday than on Friday?

(g) What was the attendance at the art show for the week?

(h) 57 of the people who attended the show were adults. How many children attended the show?

2 This picture graph shows the amount of money each friend saved.

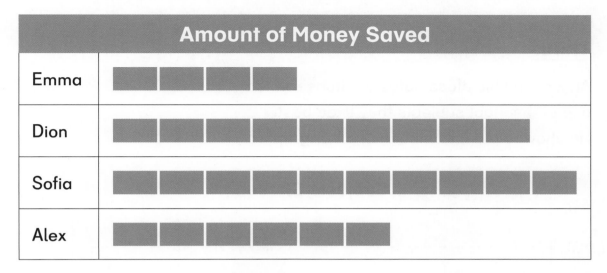

Each ▬ stands for $10.

(a) Who saved the greatest amount of money?

(b) Who saved the least amount of money?

(c) How much more money did Dion save than Alex?

(d) How much less money did Emma save than Sofia?

(e) How much money did each friend save?

(f) How much did the 4 friends save altogether?

(g) Sofia spends $25 of her savings on a game.
How much money will she have left?

(h) Mei saved $20 more than Alex.
How many ▬ would be used to add her savings to the graph?

Exercise 1 · page 141

Think

Alex asked his classmates to choose which
one of 4 school subjects they liked best.
He showed the information in a **bar graph**.

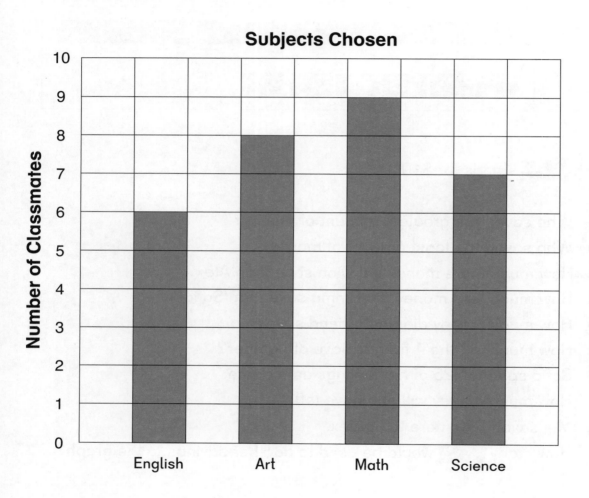

Subjects Chosen

What can you tell
from the graph?

Learn

Which subject did they choose the most?

Which subject did they choose the least?

What is the order of subjects from most popular to least popular?

I can easily see which of the 4 subjects is the most popular.

How many classmates chose each subject?

I can tell how many of Alex's classmates chose each subject.

How many fewer classmates chose Science than Math?

How many more classmates chose Math than English?

I can tell how many more liked one subject than another.

How many classmates did Alex ask in all?

I can find how many classmates Alex asked.

Do

1 This bar graph shows the number of 4 types of raptors rescued and released by a wildlife rescue society last year.

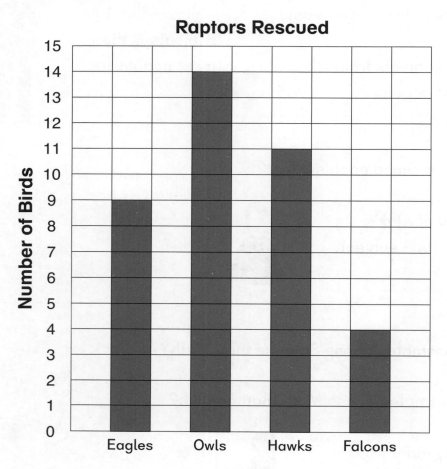

Raptors Rescued

(a) Which type of bird had the greatest number rescued?

(b) Which type of bird had the least number rescued?

(c) How many more eagles were rescued than falcons?

(d) How many of each type of bird were rescued?

(e) Turkey vultures were also rescued,
but their information is not shown on the graph.
Twice as many falcons were rescued as turkey vultures.
How many turkey vultures were rescued?

(f) How many birds, including turkey vultures,
were rescued in all?

(g) This graph shows the same information.
What is different about how the information is organized?

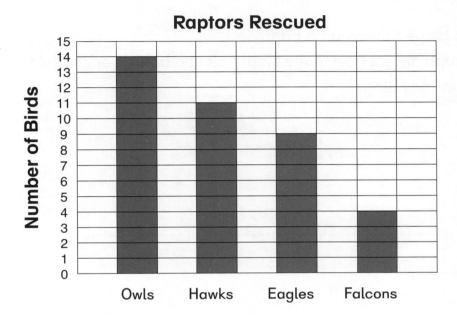

Raptors Rescued

(h) What advantage is there to organizing this information this way?

2 Mei asked her classmates which zoo exhibit they liked best and recorded the information with tally marks.

Exhibit	Tally
Reptile House	𝍷𝍷𝍷𝍷 ///
Tropical Forest	𝍷𝍷𝍷𝍷 𝍷𝍷𝍷𝍷 ////
African Savannah	𝍷𝍷𝍷𝍷 𝍷𝍷𝍷𝍷 𝍷𝍷𝍷𝍷 //
Water's Edge	𝍷𝍷𝍷𝍷 𝍷𝍷𝍷𝍷
Asian Forest	𝍷𝍷𝍷𝍷

Make a bar graph using this information.

Exercise 2 • page 145

1 Some children helped clean up a park.
This picture graph shows how many empty plastic bottles each child found and put in recycling.

Bottles Found							
Alexus	●	●	●	●	●	●	●
Daren	●	●	●				
Joshua	●	●	●	●	●		
Charlotte	●	●	●				
Mayam	●	●	●	●			

Each ● stands for 4 bottles.

(a) Who found the most bottles?
(b) Which two children found same number of bottles?
(c) How many more bottles did Alexus find than Mayam?
(d) How many fewer bottles did Daren find than Joshua?
(e) How many bottles did each of these 5 children find?
(f) Elena found 24 bottles.
   How many ● would be used to add her information to the graph?
(g) How many bottles did all 6 children, including Elena, find?

2 Brianna sold drinks at the Track and Field Day.

This picture graph shows how many of each kind she sold.

Drinks Sold at the Track and Field Day

Each ● stands for 2 drinks.

(a) Use the information in the graph to complete the table.

Number of Type of Drink Sold			
Bottled Water	Coconut Water	Electrolyte Drink	Juice
10			

(b) Which type of drink was the least popular?

(c) How many Bottled Waters and Coconut Waters did Brianna sell?

(d) How many fewer Juices did she sell than Bottled Waters?

(e) She sold the Electrolyte Drinks for $5 each.
How much money did she receive for the Electrolyte Drinks?

(f) She received $20 from selling the Bottled Waters.
What was the cost of 1 Bottled Water?

(g) How can this type of graph help Brianna decide what type of drinks to bring to the next Track and Field Day?

3 Study the bar graph and answer the questions below.

Students Who Went to the Nurse's Office This Week

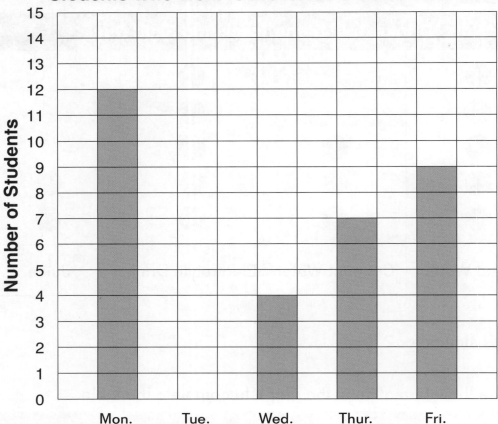

(a) On what day did the greatest number
of students go to the nurse's office?

(b) On what day did the least number
of students go to the nurse's office?

(c) How many more students went to the
nurse's office on Monday than on Wednesday?

(d) Of the total number of students who went
to the nurse's office this week, 14 had scrapes.
The rest had other injuries.
How many had other injuries?

Chapter 15

Shapes

Make pictures with shapes.

Think

Use round and straight edges to draw lines, curves, and shapes.

Learn

These are **straight** lines.

These are **curved** lines.

I used straight lines to make an open shape and a closed shape.

I made this shape. It is a closed shape with two straight sides.

Do

1 Which of the following shapes are open shapes?

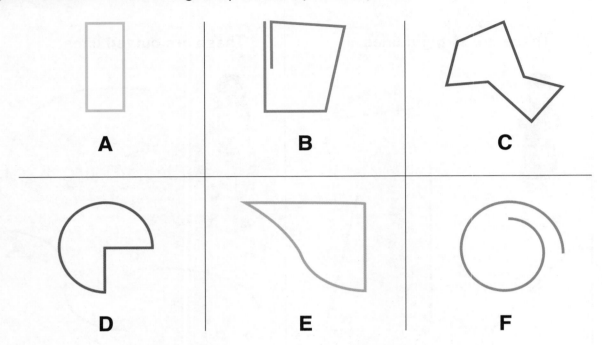

2 How many straight sides do these shapes have?

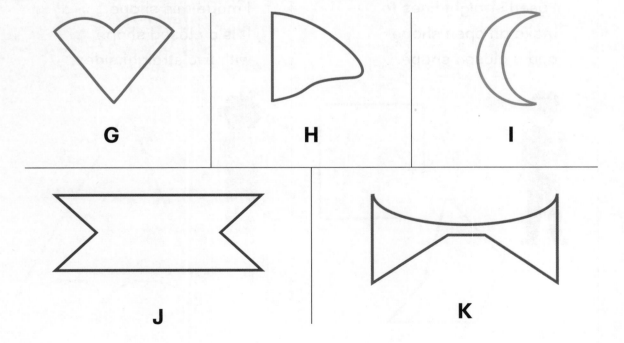

15-1 Straight and Curved Sides

3 These pictures were drawn with straight lines only.
Use a ruler to draw a picture with straight lines only.

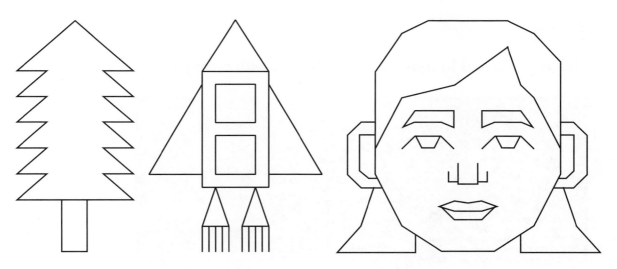

4 These pictures were drawn with straight lines and curves.
Use a ruler and a shape with a round edge to draw a picture with
straight lines and curves.

Exercise 1 • page 153

Think

Use a geoboard to make closed shapes with straight sides.

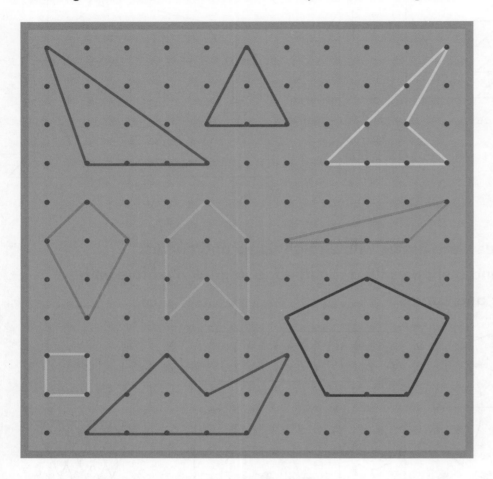

Count the number of sides and the number of corners in each shape. What can you conclude about the number of corners and sides on each?

Copy your shapes onto dot paper.

Learn

A closed shape made with straight lines is called a **polygon**.

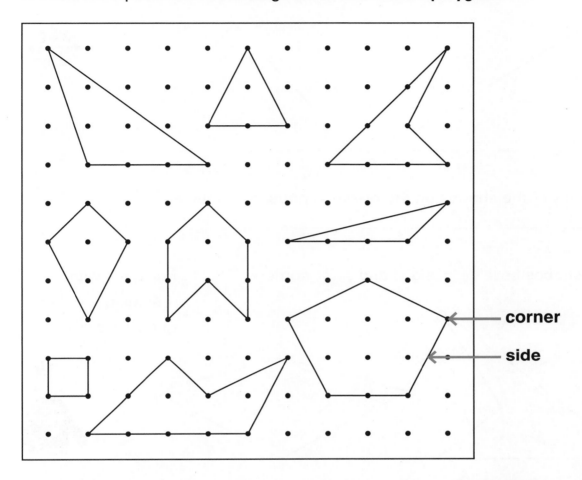

corner

side

If a figure has a curved side, or is open, it is not a polygon.

Polygons all have the same number of sides as corners.

These shapes have ▢ sides and ▢ corners.

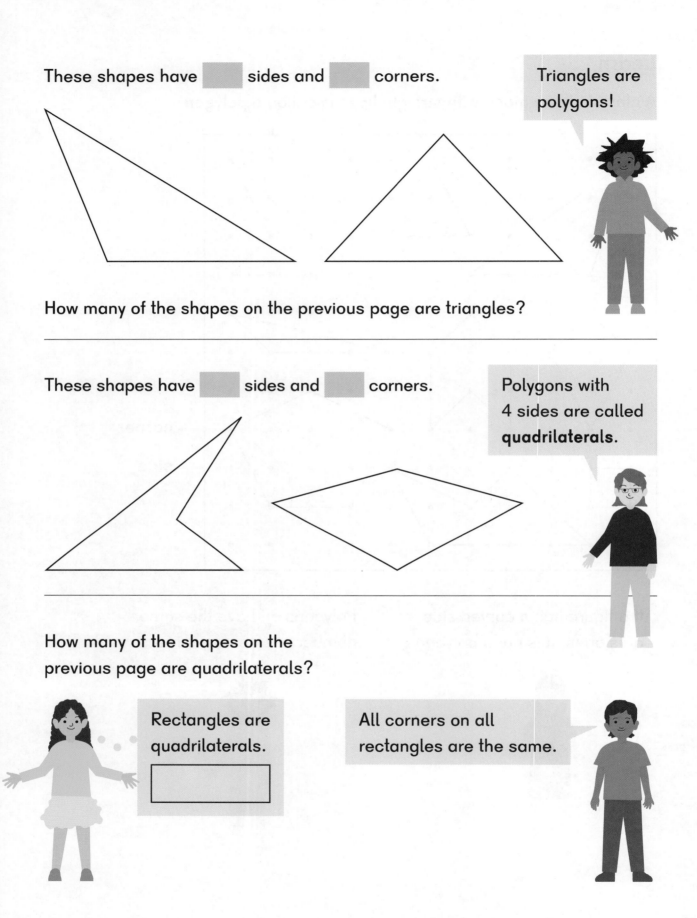

Triangles are polygons!

How many of the shapes on the previous page are triangles?

_____

These shapes have ▢ sides and ▢ corners.

Polygons with 4 sides are called **quadrilaterals**.

How many of the shapes on the previous page are quadrilaterals?

Rectangles are quadrilaterals.

All corners on all rectangles are the same.

Do

1 Which pattern block shapes are quadrilaterals?

Which shape does not have all sides of equal length?

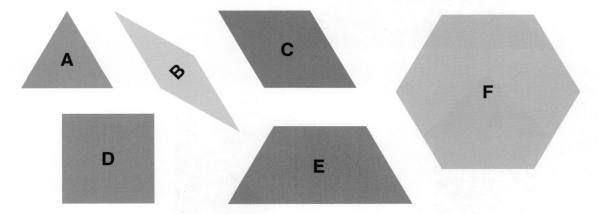

2 Use a ruler and dot paper to draw different triangles and quadrilaterals.

Which of your shapes have at least two sides the same length?

Which of them are rectangles?

Which of them are squares?

3 **Pentagons** have 5 sides.

Hexagons have 6 sides.

Which of these shapes are pentagons and which are hexagons?

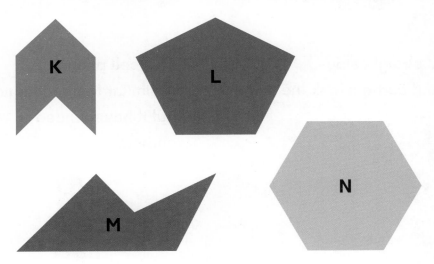

4 Put 2 tangram shapes together to make different polygons.
How many sides and corners does each shape have?

5 Look for things shaped like polygons around you.

The coin has 7 straight sides.
All the sides and corners look the same.

This cell phone
is similar to a rectangle,
but it has rounded
corners.

Exercise 2 • page 155

Think

Use circles that are the same size.
Fold one and cut it into halves.
Then fold it again and cut it into fourths.

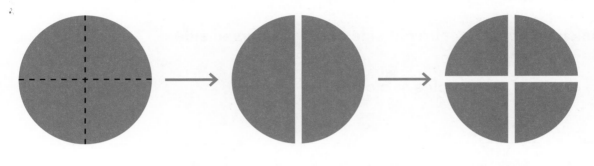

Put the fourths of a circle together to make different shapes.
Sides with equal length should line up with each other.

Learn

A half of a circle is called a **semicircle**.

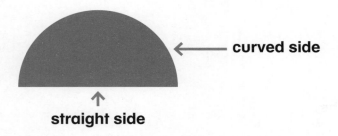

curved side

straight side

A semicircle has ☐ straight side and ☐ curved side.

There are ☐ semicircles in a circle.

A fourth of a circle is called a **quarter-circle**.

straight side → ← curved side

A quarter-circle has ☐ straight sides and ☐ curved side.

There are ☐ quarter-circles in a circle.

Compare the lengths of the sides of the quarter-circle and the semicircle.

Do

1 Start with quarter-circles and squares with straight sides
the same length as the straight sides of the quarter-circle.
Fold some of the squares in half and cut them to make triangles.

(a) Make the following shapes using
half-square triangles and quarter-circles.

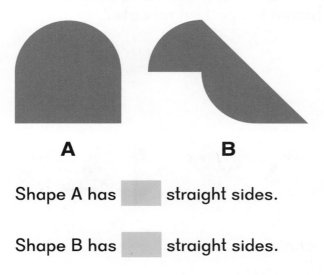

A   **B**

Shape A has [　] straight sides.

Shape B has [　] straight sides.

(b) Make other shapes from these quarter-circles and triangles.
Trace your shapes.

Exercise 3 • page 159

Lesson 4
Patterns

4

Think

Dion made this pattern with shapes.

What changes in the pattern?
How many shapes are there before the pattern repeats?
What comes next?

Learn

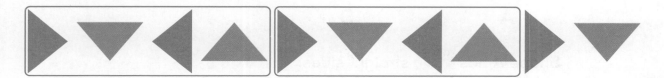

The color and the orientation changes.
The pattern repeats every ⬛ shapes.

◀ will be the next shape in the pattern.

If we rotate a shape partway,
we change its **orientation.**
The size and shape does not change.

<u>Do</u>

1 Make patterns with shapes and describe them.
What changes in the pattern?
How many shapes are there before the pattern repeats?

2 What comes next?

(a) 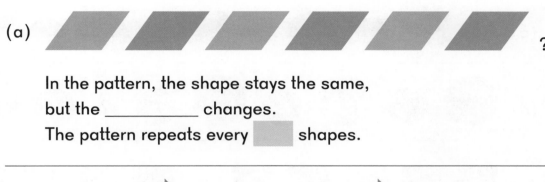 ?

In the pattern, the shape stays the same,
but the _____ changes.
The pattern repeats every ▢ shapes.

(b) 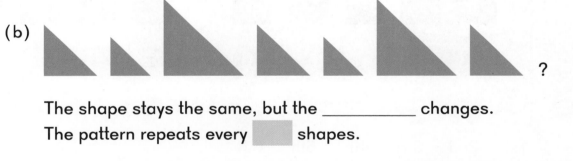 ?

The shape stays the same, but the _____ changes.
The pattern repeats every ▢ shapes.

(c) 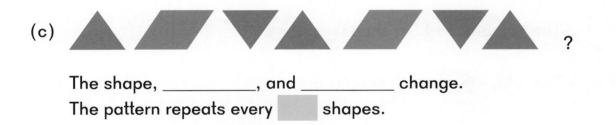 ?

The shape, _____, and _____ change.
The pattern repeats every ▢ shapes.

3 What is the missing shape in each pattern?

(a)

(b)

(c)

(d)

(e)

4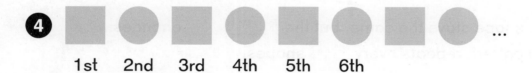

1st   2nd   3rd   4th   5th   6th

The 1st, 3rd, and 5th shapes are ▢.

The 2nd, 4th, and 6th shapes are ⬤.

(a) What is the 10th shape?

(b) What is the 15th shape?

What is the 100th shape?

5 What is the 12th shape in each pattern?

(a) ...

(b) ...

(c) ...

(d) ...

6 What is the 1st shape in each pattern?

(a) ...
| 5th | 6th | 7th | 8th | 9th |

(b) ...
| 5th | 6th | 7th | 8th | 9th | 10th |

Exercise 4 • page 163

Think

Put the objects that have similar shapes into groups.

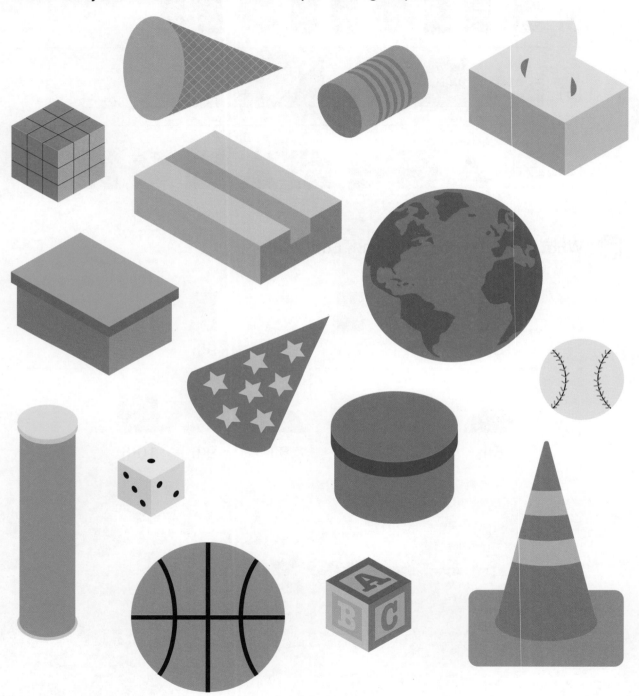

Learn

Cuboid

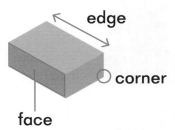

edge

corner

face

The **face** is the flat surface of a solid.
The **edge** is where 2 faces meet.
The **corner** is where 3 faces meet.

Which faces on the cuboid have the same size and shape?

A cuboid has

 faces that are rectangles,

corners, and

edges.

Cube

Cubes are cuboids in which all the faces are squares.

A cube has

faces that are squares,

corners, and

edges.

Cone

curved surface

curved edge

A cone has

☐ face that is a circle,

☐ curved surface, and

☐ curved edge.

Cylinder

A cylinder has

☐ faces that are circles,

☐ curved surface, and

☐ curved edges.

Sphere

A sphere has

☐ curved surface.

The entire surface of a sphere is curved.

Do

1 Which shape is it?

Cuboid   Cube   Cylinder   Sphere   Cone

(a) It has 2 flat faces.
It can slide or roll.
It is the _____.

(b) It cannot roll.
Its flat faces are not all the same shape.
It is the _____.

(c) It has 0 edges.
It is the _____.

(d) It has 1 edge.
It is the _____.

(e) All of its faces are the same shape.
It is the _____.

2 Look at other shapes from building blocks.
How many faces, corners, and edges does each shape have?
Look at the shapes of the faces.
Which of them can you name?

3 Put some shapes in a bag.
Feel one with your hands and describe it.
How many faces, corners, and edges does it have?
What are the shapes of the faces?
Are any of the surfaces or edges curved?
Is it a cuboid, cone, cylinder, or sphere, or some other shape?

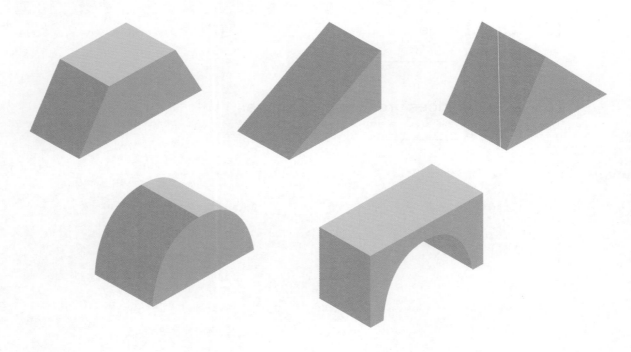

Exercise 5 • page 167

15-5 Solid Shapes

❶ Which of the following shapes are polygons?

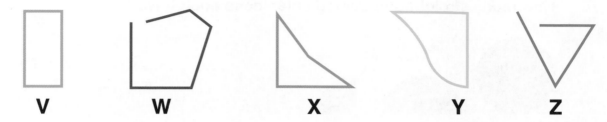

| V | W | X | Y | Z |

❷ Which of the following shapes are quadrilaterals?
Which of them have equal-length sides?

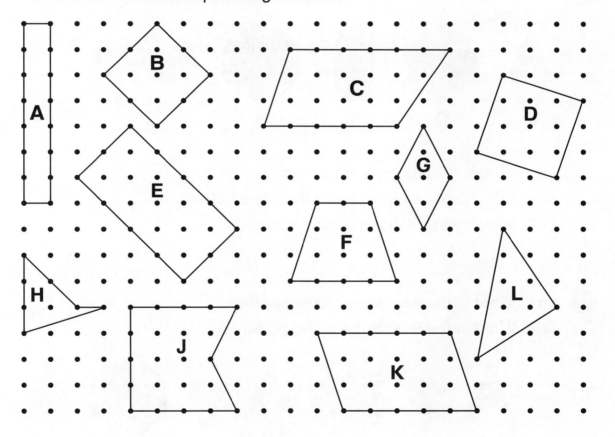

3 Draw polygons with 5, 6, 7, and 8 sides on dot paper.

4 Name each of the following shapes.
How many straight and curved sides does each have?

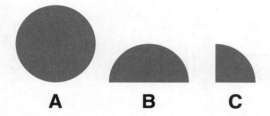

A   B   C

5 Name each of the following solids.

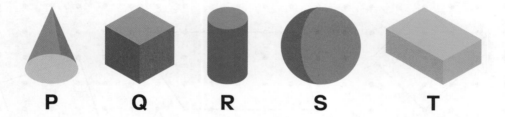

P   Q   R   S   T

(a) Which shapes have 8 corners?
(b) Which shapes have more than one flat face?
(c) Which shapes have curved surfaces?

6 (a) What is the next shape in the pattern?
(b) What is the 9th shape in the pattern?

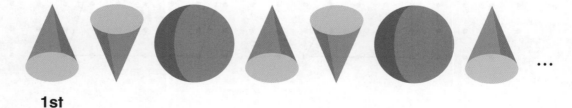

1st

Exercise 6 • page 171

1 Find the value.

(a) 708 + 224   (b) 438 + 63   (c) 246 + 381

(d) 937 – 81   (e) 623 – 218   (f) 800 – 622

(g) 544 + 381   (h) 804 – 317   (i) 487 + 255

2 Put the numbers in order from least to greatest.

(a)

| 456 | 654 | 546 | 645 |

(b)

| $\frac{1}{2}$ | $\frac{1}{5}$ | $\frac{1}{4}$ | $\frac{1}{9}$ |

3 (a) Use a ruler to measure the sides of this rectangle in centimeters.

(b) How much longer is the length than the width?

(c) If you measured the length in inches, would the number of inches be more or less than the number of centimeters?

4 Find the value.

(a) 3×4 (b) 9×5 (c) 5×6

(d) 2×8 (e) 7×10 (f) 4×8

(g) $24 \div 4$ (h) $30 \div 3$ (i) $25 \div 5$

(j) $21 \div 3$ (k) $18 \div 2$ (l) $90 \div 10$

5 A restaurant is open from 10:00 a.m. to 11:00 p.m. How many hours is it open?

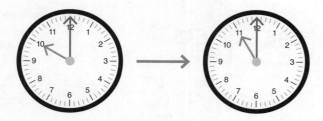

6 What fraction of each shape is colored?

(a) 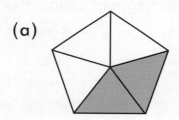 (b)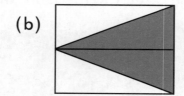

(c) 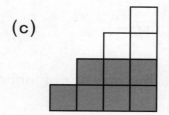 (d)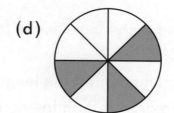

7 (a) What number is 10 more than 432?

(b) What number is 300 less than 847?

(c) What number is 60 more than 629?

(d) What number is 98 more than 287?

8
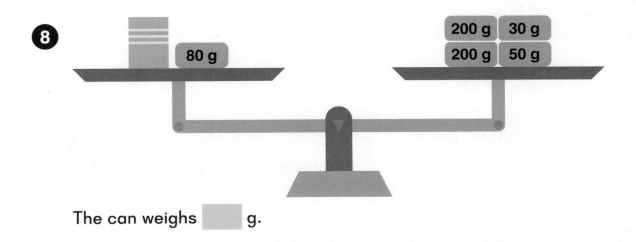

The can weighs ⬜ g.

9 Mario drew a polygon that had 10 sides. How many corners does it have?

10 What comes next in the pattern? What is the 15th shape?

1st

11 ⬤⬤⬤⬤⬤⬤ stands for 24.

What does ⬤⬤⬤⬤ stand for?

12 Kawai's tennis lesson begins at 4:30 p.m. and lasts 40 minutes.
What time does his tennis lesson end?

13 Katherine has 1 five-dollar bill, 2 one-dollar bills, 7 quarters, and 1 dime.

(a) How much money does she have?

$9.25

(b) She wants to buy this book.
How much more money does she need?

14 The total capacity of 4 identical tanks is 32 L.

(a) What is the capacity of 1 tank?

(b) What is the capacity of 3 tanks?

15 A sofa costs $746.
A coffee table costs $547 less than the sofa.

(a) How much does the coffee table cost?

(b) What is the total cost of the sofa and the coffee table?

16 Abigail has $150.
Yara has $80 more than Abigail.
How much money do they have altogether?

Exercise 7 • page 175